Loom Knitting for Little People

Whipping up amazing creations with looms and string!

BETHANY A. DAILEY

Copyright © 2011
by Bethany A. Dailey
A Gettin' It Pegged! publication in conjunction with Really Big Ideas, Inc.
http://gettinitpegged.com/

All rights reserved. No part of this publication may be reproduced, distributed, or transmitted in any form or by any means, including photocopying, recording, or other electronic or mechanical methods, without the prior written permission of the publisher.

The written instructions, photographs, designs, projects and patterns in this publication are intended for the personal, noncommercial use of the retail purchaser and are under federal copyright laws; they are not to be reproduced in any form for commercial use. Permission is granted to photocopy patterns solely for the personal use of the retail purchaser.

Permission requests may be sent to the publisher at the following address: Really Big Ideas, Inc.; 229 S. 96th Street; Tacoma, WA 98444

Author & Designer:
Bethany A. Dailey
Model Photography:
Christina A. Flores Photography
Technical Photography:
Bethany A. Dailey
Graphic Designer: Tanya Goen
Illustrators: Bethany A. Dailey and Megan J. Dailey
Project Editor: Jennifer K. Stark
Technical Advisor:
Emily R. Dailey
Models: Blake Strodemier, Bryonna Gordley, Catie F., Emily R. Dailey, Kyle O. Wright, Liam, Nora, Presley Strodemier, and Tristan McEachern

Library of Congress Cataloging-in-Publication Data available upon request.

ISBN-13:
978-0615532073
ISBN-10:
0615532071

First U.S. Edition: September 2011
10 9 8 7 6 5 4 3 2 1

Inside

3	Introduction
4	Getting Started
5	Size and gauge calculator
6	Standard measurements

7 Wearables

8	Toadally Tee Appliqué
12	Striped Pull-On Pants
15	Pocket Scarf
18	2-Piece Hooded Vest
22	Sneaker Slippers
26	So Cool Cap
29	Plush Booties
30	Pom-pom Hat
32	**Sweetheart Set**
	Hat
	Scarf
	Mittens
36	Jester Hat
40	Felted Fun Hat
44	Sporty Visor

47 Accessories

48	**Pacifier Pals**
	Binky Blossom
	Just Ducky
	Bear Buddy
54	Rwanda Wristers & Walkabout Bag
58	Lacy Heirloom Pillow
62	**Pair of Lacy Trims**
	Cabled Lacy Trim
	Lacy Scalloped Trim
67	Cozy Crib Blanket

71 Play Things

72	Felted Art Satchel
76	Koby the Striped Kitty
82	Silly Sidewinder
88	**Doll Duds**
	Bunny's Frilly Skirt
	Rosette Bunny Band
	Bear Pull-Over
	Bear Hat
	Bunny Shoes
	Bear Booties
94	Crazy Caterpillar

99 Knitty Gritty

100	Glossary & How-To's
112	Acknowledgements

INTRODUCTION

Gettin' it pegged!

What better way is there to show your love for a child, than in making something special with your own two hands? That's what this book is all about — combining our love for loom knitting with the joy of giving to those little people that are so dear to our hearts. Being able to pass along a handcrafted item that just might make a child's days a little happier, tends to make us happier too!

Some of the items in this collection have been waiting in the wings to make their official appearance. They were either created for my own girls to enjoy, or as gifts for the new generation of nieces and nephews in our family. Others were created with you in mind! I was hoping to design items that would inspire your loom-knitting imagination and provide you with projects worthy of your time and giving spirit. Maybe the next goodie you create on your looms from these pages will become that cherished heirloom, kept and loved for years to come!

There's something else about this book that I'm so excited to share with you. Not only are the pages filled with colorful incentive to share your talents with the kids in your life, but also a way to help children around the world! When you purchase this book, at least half of the earnings will be sent to help kids in need, particularly orphans needing medical care, and ultimately, help in finding their forever families through the wonderful and giving organization, ShowHope.org.

It's amazing how much we can accomplish with a little bit of string and a loom, isn't it? One stitch at a time, with each peg wrapped, together we're gettin' it pegged!

Happy Looming!

Bethany
GettinItPegged.com

GETTING STARTED

Before you pick up the loom ...

The projects you'll find in this book range from skill levels of beginner to advanced, so there's a little something for everyone. The experienced loom knitter will enjoy a range of projects to keep them inspired, while novice loomers can appreciate a challenge in developing their skills to reach the next level. You'll find the skill level noted at the top of each pattern's title page.

Many of the projects used in this book can be excellent stash busters. Feel free to reclaim what little bits and bobs you have rolling around in your yarn baskets to use for things like embellishing, embroidering, blanket stitching, you name it! Quite a few projects only require a very small amount of yardage and are perfect for finishing off those last bits of yarn left over from a larger project.

I'm a big fan of using what you have on hand. If you have a group of yarns that would make excellent coordinating stripes, but they happen to be of a different weight than the yarns called for in the pattern, make use of the **Gauge Calculator** found on Page 5 to determine how to make your stash work for you! The same concept applies to that favorite loom you'd really prefer to use, rather than the one listed in the project. It's all very simple and interchangeable. We don't have to be set in stone about any of these things. This is what creating something by hand is all about — the individual and creative touches we put into our projects. This is what makes the finished item truly unique and a little part of YOU — perfect for gifting!

As you work through the patterns, you'll find special tips in the **Makin' It Easy!** boxes. Make sure to read through each of those before starting on the pattern, to make sure that you're aware of all the things that will make creating your item much easier.

Abbreviations are used in many of the patterns in this book and a full **abbreviation key** can be found on Page 100. Also, the techniques utilized for each project can be found in the **Techniques Used** section in each pattern.

Tucked into the back section of the book is the **Glossary** and **How-To's** section. In it you'll find the description and step-by-step instructions for all the processes used throughout the book.

Because this is not necessarily an entry level loom knitting book, the more basic techniques are described briefly, with added time spent on those techniques that are more involved.

I think you'll find the detailed descriptions and close-up pictures to be especially helpful in working through the projects.

4 Loom Knitting for Little People

GETTING STARTED

Learning to adjust for size and gauge

One of the most amazing things about making things with string is that you have the freedom to show some creative initiative — do a little free-stylin' from the original pattern instructions. I love to think of patterns as the spring board from which all kinds of other things can be made. Adjusting the pattern for another size or gauge than was originally listed is the most basic form of this creative freedom. You can use any loom with any weight yarn and dive into your project with the confidence that it will turn out fantastic in the end!

This page gives you the headache-free, surefire way to adjust your patterns for another gauge and/or size. It's really easy-peasy, I promise!

It all begins with a swatch. You'll create a sample of the project you will be looming, with the yarn and loom choices you plan to use in creating your project. Make sure you cast on enough stitches and knit enough rows to create a swatch of at least three to four inches square. This will give you an excellent source for averaging stitches and rows per inch. Make sure to work your swatch in the same stitch style that is used in the original pattern — all knit, ribbing, garter stitch, etc.

Count the number of stitches and rows per inch in your swatch. It is helpful to use two to four of those inches as a total count. Make sure to count partial stitches as well! They add up over several inches and can make a big difference in the size of the finished piece. You would then divide this number by the number of inches you counted, to end up with an accurate count of your swatch's number of stitches/rows per inch.

You will then plug your numbers into the Gauge Calculator chart below.

At this point, it's just a simple math calculation. The important thing to remember is that you will need to do the calculation in the shaded boxes each time there is a new stitch or row count listed in the pattern. This will keep all of your proportions correct. You will find the correct numbers to plug into the chart listed in each pattern's gauge information. For example:

3.5 sts (S) x 6 rows (R) per 1"

When adjusting your pattern for size, you will measure the width and length required for the finished item. Each significant width and length variance will need to be measured. As an example, the Toadally Tee Appliqué (Page 8) has several different widths in its design. You would want to consider each place where the width changes, and plug those numbers into the Size Calculator chart below.

Size Calculator

Width needed (in inches)	x	S	=	New size's peg count
Length needed (in inches)	x	R	=	New size's row count

If you plan on changing both the size and the gauge of a pattern, you will first convert all row and stitch numbers to the new size. These new numbers will then be plugged into the Gauge Calculator chart in the S and R spots. You would then proceed to figure out your gauge conversion based on your new size.

There is really nothing more to it! It's a simple matter of measuring, plugging the numbers into the charts, and then performing the basic calculations listed. You now have the tools and freedom to make most anything, no matter which size you need, what yarn you're using, or which loom you're working on. Isn't that a terrific feeling?

Gauge Calculator

Your sts (per inch)	÷	Pattern's sts per inch (S)	=	Your conversion number for sts	x	Each st count in pattern	=	New gauge's peg count
Your rows (per inch)	÷	Pattern's rows per inch (R)	=	Your conversion number for rows	x	Each row count in pattern	=	New gauge's row count

GETTING STARTED

Standard measurements

Following are several sizing charts. When sizing garments, the fit is based on actual measurements, plus ease (additional inches or centimeters). The first chart entitled "Fit" recommends the amount of ease to add to body measurements if you prefer a close-fitting garment, an oversized garment, or something in-between. For individual body differences, changes can be made in body and lengths when appropriate. However, consideration must be given to the project pattern. Certain sizing changes may alter the appearance of a garment. *Source: Craft Yarn Council's www.YarnStandards.com*

How to measure

1. Chest/Bust

Measure around the fullest part of the chest/bust. Do not draw the tape too tightly.

2. Center Back Neck–to-Cuff

With arm slightly bent, measure from back base of neck across shoulder around bend of elbow to wrist.

3. Back Waist Length

Measure from the most prominent bone at base of neck to the natural waistline.

4. Cross Back

Measure from shoulder to shoulder.

5. Sleeve Length

With arm slightly bent, measure from armpit to cuff.

More online

Bev's Country Cottage also has an excellent online resource for general measurement guidelines, especially geared toward crafting for babies and children here: http://bevscountrycottage.com/size-chart.html

Fit *(all measurements in inches)*

Very-close fitting: Use actual chest/bust measurement or less
Close-fitting: Add 1–2" **Standard-fitting:** Add 2–4"
Loose-fitting: Add 4–6" **Oversized:** Add 6" or more

Baby's size:	3 mos.	6 mos.	12 mos.	18 mos.	24 mos.
Chest	16	17	18	19	20
Center Back Neck-to-Cuff	10 ½	11 ½	12 ½	14	18
Back Waist Length	6	7	7 ½	8	8 ½
Cross Back (Shoulder to shoulder)	7 ¼	7 ¾	8 ¼	8 ½	8 ¾
Sleeve Length to Underarm	6	6 ½	7 ½	8	8 ½
Height	25	26	27	28	31

Child's size:	2	4	6	8	10	12	14	16
Chest	21	23	25	26 ½	28	30	31 ½	32 ½
Center Back Neck-to-Cuff	18	19 ½	20 ½	22	24	26	27	28
Back Waist Length	8 ½	9 ½	10 ½	12 ½	14	15	15 ½	16
Cross Back (Shoulder to shoulder)	9 ¼	9 ¾	10 ¼	10 ¾	11 ¼	12	12 ¼	13
Sleeve Length to Underarm	8 ½	10 ½	11 ½	12 ½	13 ½	15	16	16 ½
Height	35	41	47	50	55	58	60	61

Head sizing

	Premie	Baby	Toddler	Child	Woman	Man
Circumference	12"	14"	16"	18"	20"	22"

Sock sizing

Child's shoe size	0-4	4-8	7-11	10-2	2-6
Sock size	4-5	5-6 ½	6-7 ½	7-8 ½	8-9 ½

Ages	6-12 mo.	1-3 y.	3-5y.	5-9y.	7-13y.
Foot circumference (Around widest part of foot)	4 ½	5 ½	6	6 ½	7
Sock height (From where heel meets the floor to top of sock)	2 ½	3 ½	4 ½	5 ½	6 ½
Total foot length (Along the bottom of foot, from back of heel to longest toe)	4	5	6	7 ½	8

wearables

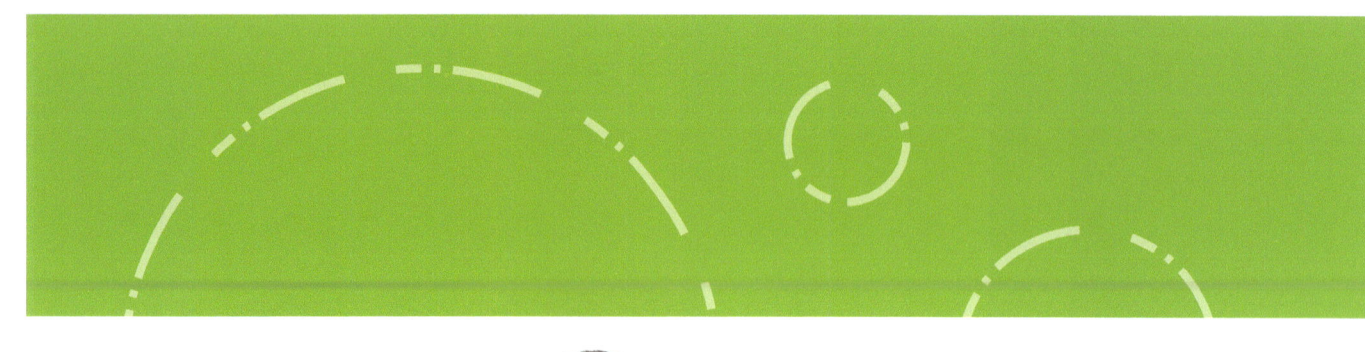

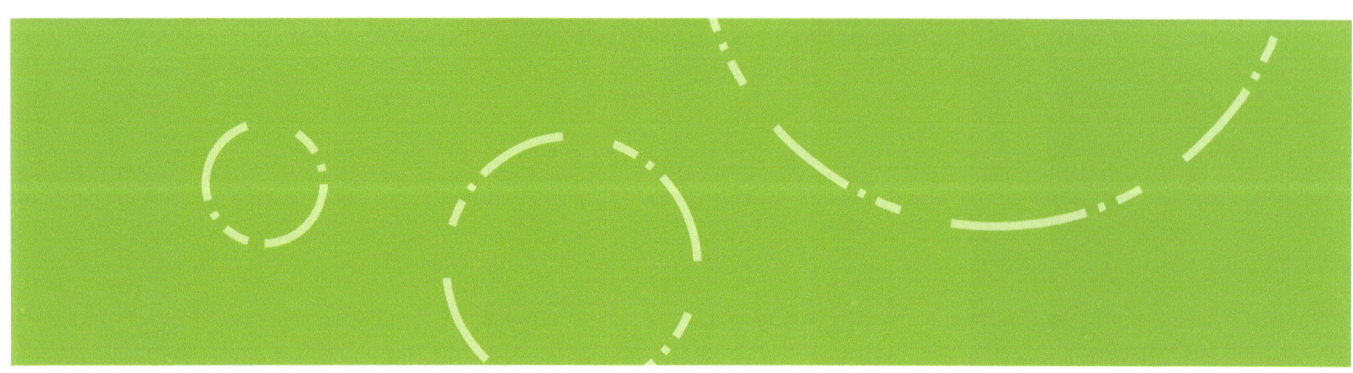

Toadally Tee Appliqué

Somebody once said that it wasn't easy being green but, I think this guy has no end of fun and leisurely days, getting to hang out on the front of your child's tee — or back pack or pillow or anywhere else he finds a pad to land! This froggy is made to be perched wherever you want him, and you can personalize his surrounding details any way you wish.

Finished size
8.5" high; 5" across widest point

Gauge
3.5 sts (S) x 6 rows (R) per inch
See Gauge and Size Calculators, Page 5

Needed
- Large-gauge loom with at least 19 pegs; one side of a green long 50-peg Knifty Knitter was used in sample.
- #5 Bulky yarn in 5 colors, approx. ¼th skein (or less) of each: Patons Shetland Chunky in leaf green, dark leaf green, aran, rich teal, and russet used in sample; 75% acrylic, 25% wool, 121 yards per skein.
- Loom tool, 5.5 mm crochet hook, tapestry needle, sewing needle and thread, straight pins, flexible/washable fabric glue.

Notes
Techniques used: U-Stitch/Flat Knit, Purl, Panel Knitting, Half Hitch, Crochet CO, Basic BO, Increasing, Decreasing, Seaming, Basic Sewing Skills.

This pattern uses one strand of yarn held throughout.

All Knits are worked as U-Stitches/Flat Knits throughout.

Step by step
Using the main frog-colored yarn, CCO 9 pegs, making the loops centered on the loom. Leave a 12" CO tail for seaming later. Work as a flat panel.

Row 1: S1, K8.

Rows 2-5: S1, K remaining pegs, M1 (M1 = move last peg's loop over 1 to the outside of knitted panel. Pull connecting line up from previous row and place over newly emptied peg.)

You will now have 13 pegs filled on your loom.

Rows 6-12: S1, K12.

Row 13: HH onto 2 additional pegs before main sts. S1, K14. HH onto 2 additional pegs after main sts. You should now have 17 pegs filled.

Row 14: S1, K16.

Row 15: HH onto 1 additional peg before main sts. S1, K17. HH onto 1 additional peg after main sts. You should now have a total of 19 pegs filled.

Rows 16 & 17: S1, K18.

Rows 18-27: Dec1 at WY side. S1, K remaining pegs. You should have 9 pegs filled after row 27.

Row 28: BBO first peg. K7. BBO last peg.

Row 29: HH onto 2 additional pegs before main sts. S1, K8. HH onto 2 additional pegs after main sts. You should now have 11 pegs filled.

Row 30: S1, K10

Rows 31 & 32: HH onto 1 additional peg before main sts. S1, K remaining pegs. You should have 13 pegs filled after row 32.

Toadally Tee Appliqué, cont.

Rows 33-49: S1, K12.

BBO all sts.

Using CO tail, create a running st between the eyes and gather to create two large froggy eye shapes. Knot to secure.

Using a contrasting colored yarn, create the details of the frog. The mouth and leg details were top chained with a crochet hook, but a backstitch embroidery stitch would work as well.

The frog is then outlined, including between the eyes, with either a crochet slip st, or a blanket st.

With your eye-colored yarn, you can either crochet two 1½" circles and stitch them onto place in the eye area, or you can embroider them on. After the white circles are in place, add the pupil detail as in the illustration.

Weave in all ends and trim close to work.

It's a good idea to steam block the frog so it will lay flat and even.

Pin frog onto your item (in this case a tee-shirt). Stitch into place using sewing thread and needle. Make sure the tee stays straight as you're stitching so it won't pucker.

Tongue

The tongue was created using the following crochet method. (If you're not comfortable with a crochet hook, an I-Cord about 8" in length would work great, too.):

Using crochet hook, chain 5 sts.

Turn and crochet slip st back to beginning yarn tail, inserting hook through the top loops of each chain.

Grab beginning yarn tail and hold it along with WY, so you are using 2 strands as 1, and chain until you reach the end of the yarn tail. Continue to chain with just the WY strand until you've reached your desired tongue length. Fasten off and weave in ends.

However you create your tongue, attach it to the tee using flexible, washable fabric glue.

MAKIN' IT EASY!

Once the frog himself is created, you can put him in any surroundings you choose! It would be super fun to have your child use fabric markers and paints to create a swampy setting for the frog to find a home in, lily pads and all — or any other toad-ally terrific backgrounds you can think of!

Fly

The fly is also created using just a few crochet sts:

Leaving a long yarn tail, chain 3 sts.

Slip st into first chain created, to form a small oval. Fasten off, leaving a long yarn tail for stitching your fly's curly flight trail.

The fly is then stitched in place onto the shirt using your sewing thread and needle. Use the beginning yarn tail to form wing shapes that are stitched at the sides of the oval. Use the long ending yarn tail to create a curly flight path for your fly. You may find it easier to use your flexible fabric glue to secure the wings and curly flight tail in place. You can also tie a knot at the end of the trail, to keep the yarn from separating, and to let the trimmed ends beyond the knot fluff away from the shirt, unglued, for a fun 3-D effect.

Follow the fabric glue manufacturer's instructions for drying time and washing methods.

ELSEWHERE IN THE BOOK …
Make it a set!

Sneaker Slippers, **Page 22**

Striped Pull-On Pants, **Page 12**

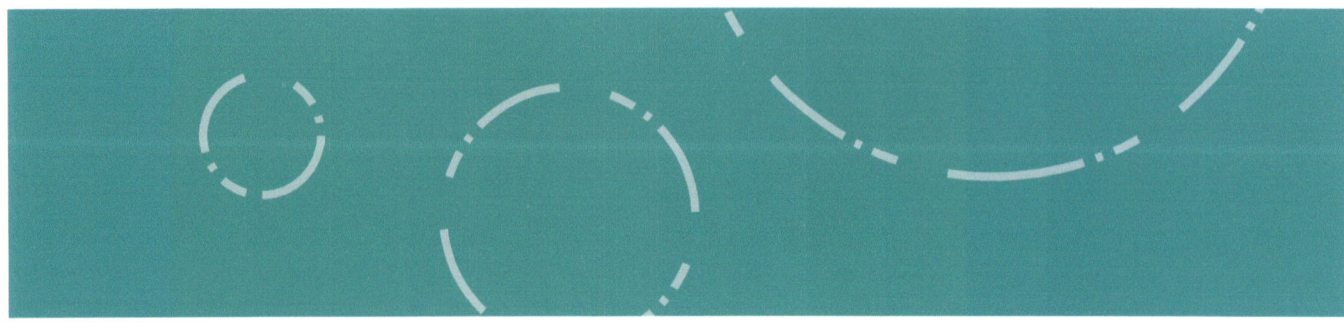

Striped Pull-On Pants

MODERATE

5 BULKY

The elements of these knit pants make them such a great project to create for little ones. They have a stretchable waistband for easy wearing, and the ankle cuffs keep those pant legs up so there's no tripping. With the added insert, right where the most stretch is needed, your toddlers can do what they do best: crawl, bend, squat, and stretch! Both of my great-nephews have gotten to wear them and each of them seemed to think that the comfort along with the happy stripes made playtime extra fun!

Finished size

This pattern is sized to fit a toddler size 12-24 months, depending on the child.

18" high; 10.5" across widest point;
21" waist circumference;
10" leg circumference.

Gauge

3.5 sts (**S**) x 6 rows (**R**) per inch

See Gauge and Size Calculators, Page 5

Needed

- Large-gauge loom with at least 34 pegs: Sample uses yellow long 38-peg Knifty Knitter and loom clips.
- #5 Bulky yarn in 6 colors, approx. ½ skein of each: Patons Shetland Chunky in leaf green, dark leaf green, soft teal, rich teal, mustard, and russet used in sample; 75% acrylic, 25% wool, 121 yds per skein.
- Elastic sewing thread: Sample uses 1 pkg Stretchrite in black; approx. 30 yds
- Loom tool, 5.5 mm crochet hook, tapestry needle, pins for seaming.

Notes

Techniques used: U-Stitch, Purl, Panel Knitting, Crochet CO, Adjustable CO, Basic BO, Increasing, Decreasing, K2tog, Seaming.

This pattern uses one strand of yarn held throughout.

All Knits and PFK are worked as U-Stitches throughout.

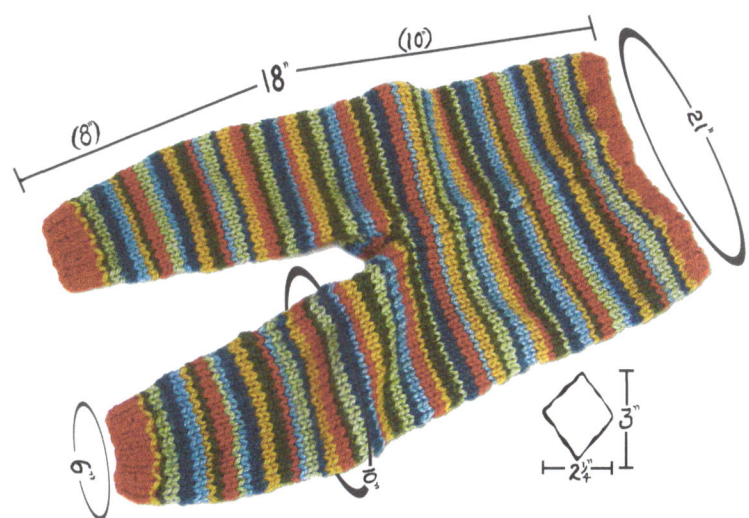

MAKIN' IT EASY!

When using the elastic thread, make sure to keep a constant, stretched tension while knitting. This will make sure that the elastic will be able to form fit while it is worn, as well as stretch to the width of the regular knitted yarn. Just hold the elastic strand taut, while holding the yarn strand as you normally would during knitting. It's a little tricky at first, but the technique does become easier with practice.

Step by steps

Note: You will be making two of the following set of instructions. One will become the right side of the pants, and the other will become the left side. The project is worked from the waistband down to the ankle cuff on each piece.

Set your loom clips into a 34-peg configuration on your loom, for more even tension throughout. Holding waistband/ankle cuff colored yarn together with the elastic thread (see Makin' it Easy!), CCO 34 pegs. Leave a 12" CO tail for seaming later. Work as a flat panel.

Striped Pull-On Pants, cont.

Rows 1-5: *K2, P2 ... Repeat from * to end of row.

Tie elastic thread securely and trim to 4".

Rows 6-60: K all pegs. Work in a random stripe pattern, using your 6 yarn colors (sample uses a combination of 1- and 2-row stripes).

Rows 60-76 (54 rows): Join to work a pant leg in the round. K34, continuing the random stripes.

Rows 77-100 (24 rows): Follow the instructions below, working Right Leg in one panel, and Left Leg in the other panel. Dec1 every other row at inside seam:

  Right Leg: Make the dec. at the last peg worked (move 2nd to last peg's loop to last peg, K2tog in next row. Adjust sts and clips as necessary.)

  Left Leg: Make the dec. at the first peg worked (move 2nd peg's loop to 1st peg, K2tog in next row. Adjust sts and clips as necessary.)

Rows 101-108 (8 rows): Add elastic thread to WY and work two strands held as one (see Makin' It Easy!). *K2, P2 ... repeat from * to end of row.

BBO all pegs. Make sure elastic thread is tied securely so that it doesn't unravel.

Follow all of the steps above to make another panel, keeping the stripes identical. Make sure to follow the separate Right and Left Leg instructions when called for.

Crotch insert

CCO 3 pegs. Follow the stripe pattern found at the point of the leg opening at the crotch, and continuing in an upward direction toward the waistband. Work as a flat panel.

Row 1: K3.

Rows 2-6: K1, M1, K remaining pegs. (M1= increase one st each row at WY side: move the loop from the last peg over one, away from your knitting. Pull connecting line from the previous row up onto empty peg. K new loop in the same row it was created in.) You should have 8 pegs filled after row 6.

Rows 7-10: K8.

Note: At this point, you will follow the stripe pattern back down toward the bottom leg opening at the crotch. It should be a mirror image of the stripes you've just worked.

WORKING WITH STRIPES

When creating stripes, it helps to have all your skeins in a tub or basket, with extra room to maneuver the skeins. There is no need to cut strands in between stripes. When you grab a new color for the next stripe, make sure it is free from tangles with the other skeins and that the skein is pulled up and around the outside of all the other color strands, wrapping them all in place. It is also helpful to tighten any slack that may have accrued in the previous sts at the last row the new color was knitted, so that the tension remains even. Make sure to pull up the new color with tension, but not so much that it causes your work to pucker — a balance similar to "not too hot; not too cold."

Rows 11-14: K8.

Rows 15-19: K1, D1, K remaining pegs. (D1: decrease one peg at the beginning of each row: move the loop from peg 2 to peg 1. K2tog in same row.) You should have 3 pegs remaining after row 19.

Row 20: K3.

BBO all sts.

Pin the crotch piece in place with the stripes matching up. You will be stitching one half of the piece at the right leg's opening and the other half of the piece to the left leg's opening. Using a length of yarn on a yarn needle, stitch the crotch insert in place and continue up both the front and back body seams, making sure all the stripes are kept even. You can use the waistband tails left from before to complete the seaming at the top of the band for an invisible seam.

Weave in all ends and trim close to work.

Lightly block and let the striped fun begin!

Pocket Scarf

 BEGINNER  SUPER BULKY

I have to admit that this project has been a long time coming. My daughter, Megan, devised the idea and was very insistent I make one for her. Time happens and other things get pushed to the top of the list, but finally, using her specifications, the Pocket Scarf was born — and oh, was it worth it! This scarf is so cozy; just the right thing to snuggle in, with hands toasty warm, nestled deep inside the pockets — and still room enough for an MP3 player, a must for a stylin' kid these days!

Finished size
62" in length x 10" wide

Gauge
2.5 sts (S) x 3.5 rows (R) per inch

See Gauge and Size Calculators, Page 5

Needed
- Large-gauge loom with at least 24 pegs; blue round 24-peg Knifty Knitter loom used in sample.
- #6 Super Bulky Weight yarn: 3 skeins: Wool Ease Thick & Quick in Navy used in sample, 80% acrylic, 20% wool, 108 yards per skein.
- Loom tool, crochet hook, tapestry needle

If you'd like the scarf to be lined, as in sample, you'll also need:
- 1 yard of 48" wide soft fabric (fleece was used in sample)
- Embroidery floss and needle

Notes
Techniques used: E-Wrap, Purl, Crochet CO, Basic BO, Seaming, Blanket Stitch.

This pattern uses one strand of yarn held throughout.

Step by step

Crochet CO 24 pegs. Work as a flat panel.

For the Border, work in the following pattern:

Row 1: EW24

Row 2: P24

Rows 3 & 5: Repeat Row 1

Rows 4 & 6: Repeat Row 2

For the Main Body, repeat the following 2-row pattern for 216 rows:

Row 1: EW24

Row 2: P4, EW 16, P4

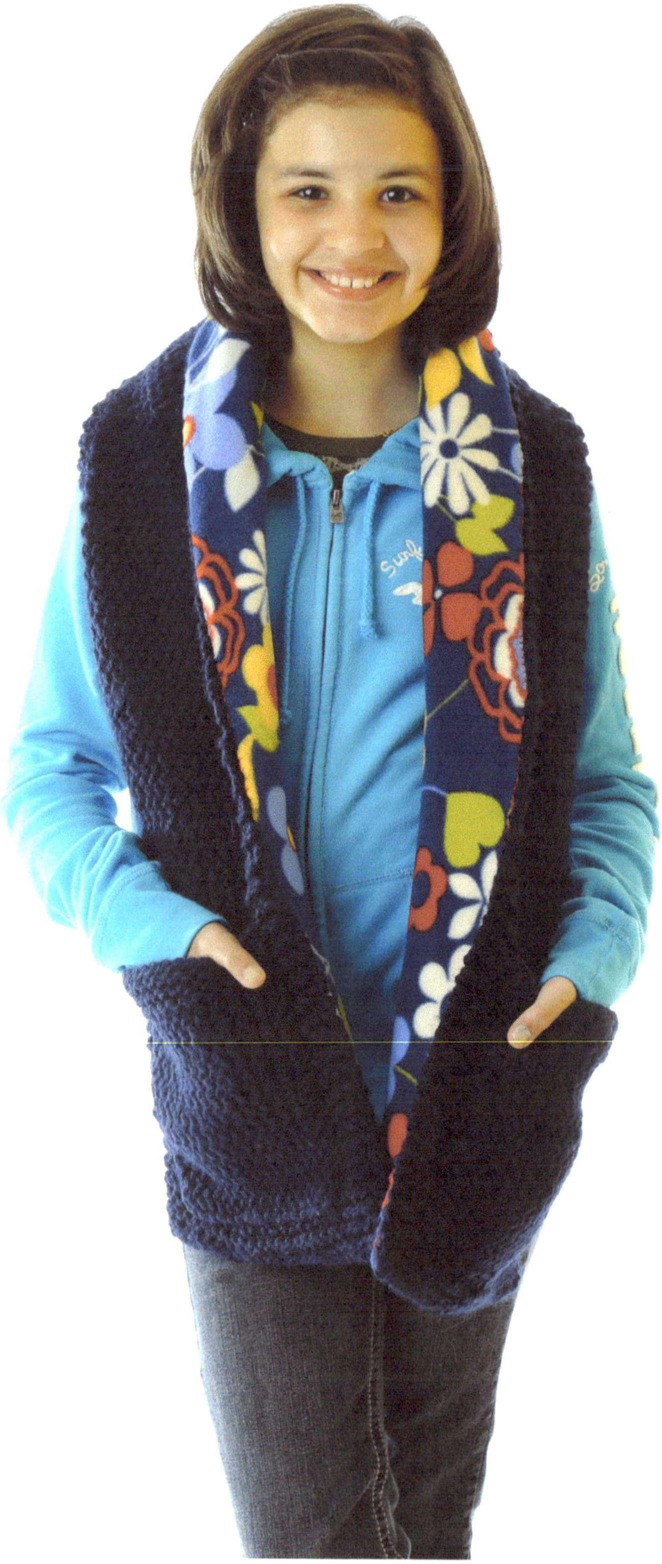

Pocket Scarf, cont.

Repeat Border steps, detailed above.

BBO all pegs.

Pockets

Crochet CO 18 pegs. Work as a flat panel.

Row 1: Sl, EW17

Row 2: S1, P16, EW1

Rows 3 & 5: Repeat Row 1

Rows 4 & 6: Repeat Row 2

Rows 7-31: S1, EW17

BBO all pegs. Make sure to leave a long enough tail to use in stitching the pocket to the scarf.

Make two.

Stitch the pockets inside the border edges, one at each end of the scarf. Weave in all ends. Block lightly.

If you'd like to line your scarf, cut your fabric into 2 sections of 33" x 12" (or the measurement required to fit your size scarf, plus 2"). This will allow you to tuck 1" of your raw edges under while seaming.

Pin fabric onto the inside of your scarf, with raw edges tucked under. Using your embroidery thread and needle, blanket stitch in place.

You will need to stitch the 2 halves of the liner together at the center line of the scarf. The sample uses a blanket stitch for this as well. Another option would be to stack the liner pieces with right sides together, before pinning to scarf. Proceed to stitch pieces together at one short end, 1" from the edge. The liner is now in one piece that can be pinned and stitched to the scarf as stated above.

Lightly steam press folded edges of liner.

2-Piece Hooded Vest

MODERATE-ADVANCED   SUPER BULKY 6

How cool is this?! You can create this absolutely adorable hooded vest in only two pieces! Want pockets? Then you can make it in four. This project is the next progression of the Pocket Scarf, which makes it even more fun! Loomed in super bulky yarn, what kid wouldn't want to cuddle up in such cozy comfort and warmth?

Finished size

This pattern is written for size 12-18 months.

12" wide x 12" from shoulder to bottom, hood: 10" from point to back shoulder seam.

Gauge

2.5 sts (**S**) x 3.5 rows (**R**) per inch

See Gauge and Size Calculators, Page 5

Needed

- **Front Panel and Hood:** Large-gauge loom with at least 24 pegs: blue round 24-peg Knifty Knitter loom used in sample.
- **Back Panel:** Large-gauge loom with at least 28 pegs: purple round 48-peg Knifty Knitter loom used in sample.
- **#6 Super Bulky Weight yarn:** MC- 2.5 skeins of Lion Brand Hometown USA in Monterey Lime used in sample; CC- 1 skein of Lion Brand Hometown USA in San Diego Navy used in sample; 100% acrylic, 81 yards per skein.
- Loom tool, crochet hook, tapestry needle, 2 peg markers, sewing thread and needle
- 5 large decorative buttons (sample uses buttons of 1¼" in diameter)

Notes

Techniques used: E-Wrap, Purl, Crochet CO, Half Hitch, Basic BO, Seaming, Basic Sewing Skills.

This pattern uses one strand of yarn held throughout.

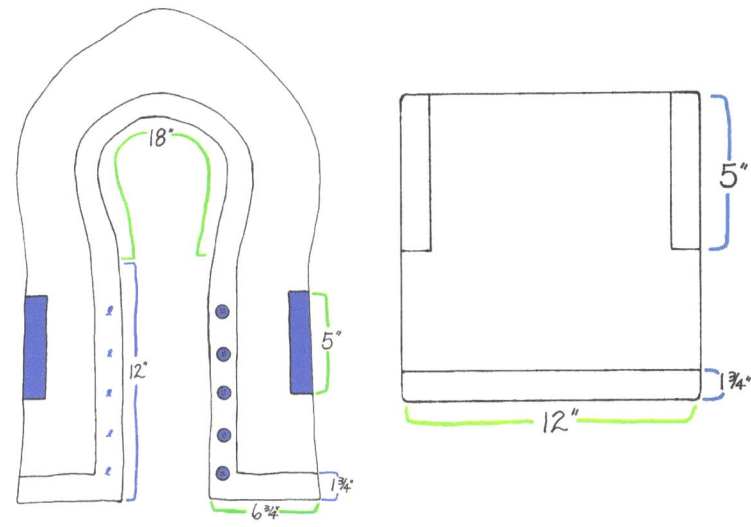

Step by step

Front panel and hood

You will begin working from left to right. Using CC, Crochet CO 16 pegs to work as a flat panel.

Place a peg marker on pegs 4 and 13. These will help you keep track of where to create your button and sleeve borders.

Rows 1-6: Repeat the following 2-row pattern:

> **Row a:** EW16
>
> **Row b:** P16

Rows 7-24 (18 rows): Repeat the following 2-row pattern:

> **Row a:** CC-EW4, twist MC over CC, MC-EW12
>
> **Row b:** MC-EW12, twist CC over MC, CC-P4

Rows 25-42 (18 rows): You will now be adding the sleeve border, using CC. You can either use an additional small ball of CC to accomplish this, or a separate skein: Repeat the following 2-row pattern:

> **Row a:** CC-EW4, twist MC over CC, MC: EW8, twist CC over MC, CC-EW4
>
> **Row b:** CC-P4, twist MC over CC, MC: EW18, twist CC over MC, CC-P4

2-Piece Hooded Vest, cont.

Rows 43-60 (18 rows): Repeat Rows 7-24

Row 61: CC-EW4, twist MC over CC, MC-EW12, Half Hitch CO 3 additional pegs for a total of 19 being worked.

Rows 62-123 (62 rows): Repeat the following 2-row pattern:

> **Row a:** MC-EW15, twist CC over MC, CC-P4
>
> **Row b:** CC-EW4, twist MC over CC, MC-EW15

Row 124: BBO 3 pegs for a total of 16 pegs remaining, MC-EW12, twist CC over MC, CC-P4

Rows 125-142 (18 rows): Repeat Rows 7-24

The next group of rows will be dealing with creating buttonholes inside the CC border. Buttonholes are worked over 2 rows and will always begin going in the direction of right to left. In order to make a buttonhole, use the following steps, which refer to the 4 pegs of the CC border:

Move each of the loops from peg 1 and peg 2 over one peg to the right, so that peg 2 is now empty and you are now using a temporary peg added to the original 4.

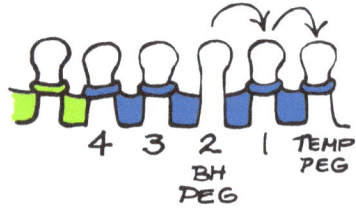

EW5, KO all but peg 2. Continue with row as directed.

On the return row, when you reach the CC border, you will purl pegs 4 and 3. Release EW from peg 2, undo twist and place on peg 1 above existing loop. Purl the 2 loops together and place this new loop back on peg 2. Purl the loop on the temporary peg and move this loop back to peg 1. You will now be back to the original 4 pegs of the CC border.

Rows 143-160 (18 rows): Repeat Rows 25-42; Add a buttonhole at each of the designated rows on the buttonhole chart.

Rows 161-178 (18 rows): Repeat Rows 7-24; Add a buttonhole at each of the designated rows on the buttonhole chart.

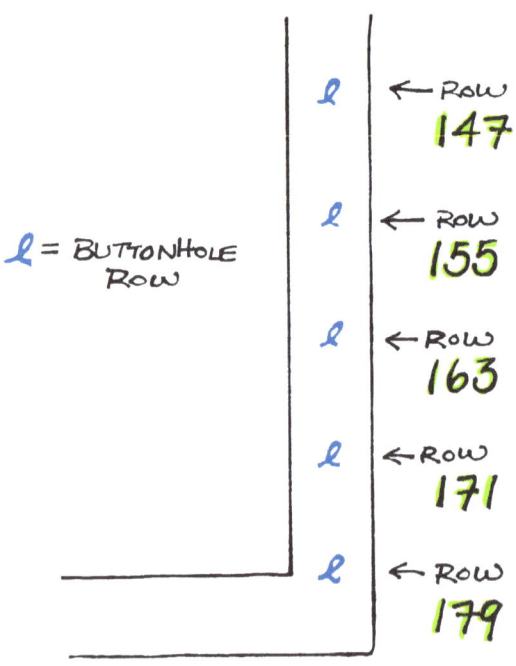

2-Piece Hooded Vest, cont.

Rows 179-184 (6 rows): Repeat Rows 1-6; Add a buttonhole at each of the designated rows on the buttonhole chart. BBO all pegs.

Back panel

Using CC, Crochet CO 28 pegs to work as a flat panel.

Place a peg marker on peg 4 and 25. This will help you keep track of where to create your sleeve borders.

Rows 1-6: Repeat the following 2-row pattern:

    Row a: EW28

    Row b: P28

Rows 7-24 (18 rows): MC- EW28

Rows 25-42 (18 rows): You will now be adding the sleeve border CC. You can either use an additional small ball of CC to accomplish this, or a separate skein: Repeat the following 2-row pattern:

    Row a: CC-EW4, twist MC over CC, MC- EW20, twist CC over MC, CC-EW4

    Row b: CC- P4, twist MC over CC, MC- EW20, twist CC over MC, CC-P4

BBO all pegs.

Pockets (Make 2)

If you'd like to add pockets to your vest, you can either create outside pockets using the same directions as in the Pocket Scarf (adjusting row/peg numbers as needed for your size), or you can create pocket inserts at the sides of the vest, as is shown in the sample.

For inside pockets:

Using MC, Crochet CO 12 pegs to work as a flat panel.

Rows 1-12: EW all pegs

BBO all pegs, leaving enough tail for seaming onto vest.

Assembly

Fold the Front Panel in half lengthwise and pin the MC side of the hood edges together. Seam along the portion where there were added stitches from Rows 61-124. Make the seam from the point of the hood, downward.

At the base of the hood seam, make a running stitch along the extra width portion and gather to pull more in

line with the rest of the panel. Knot to secure.

Pin Back Panel together with Front Panel, at the top of the arm holes and across shoulders, keeping the top edges of CC at armhole sections even.

Seam from the top of one arm hole, across the shoulders, finishing with the second arm hole. The gathered section of the hood should be at the center of the seam. Make sure to keep checking that each arm hole and hood section remains even as you seam.

If you're using inside pockets, pin them in place on the inside of the front sections, placed inside the MC edges before the CC borders. Place one edge of the pocket so it is even with the MC edge that has the arm holes. Using long BO tails, stitch invisibly in place on all sides except at edge with arm holes.

Pin side edges together and stitch, making sure to stitch pocket to Back Panel at edge, not Front. You can leave the bottom border section open for a decorative accent.

Weave in all ends and trim.

To stitch the decorative buttons in place, lay the front panel with the buttonholes over the opposite CC border panel, just as if you were going to button up the vest. Mark the places under the buttonholes with pins. This is a great way to make sure the buttons end up in the correct places. Stitch your buttons securely in place at the pins.

Block lightly to help make all those stitches comfortable in their new positions.

Sneaker Slippers

MODERATE-ADVANCED

MEDIUM

I remember owning a pair of tennis-shoe roller skates when I was a kid. I absolutely loved the novelty of wearing items on my feet that looked like sneakers, but were actually something else entirely. This project reminds me of the days when you could still buy penny candy at the corner store, enjoy Saturday morning cartoons, and when it was still such a riot to be the trickster!

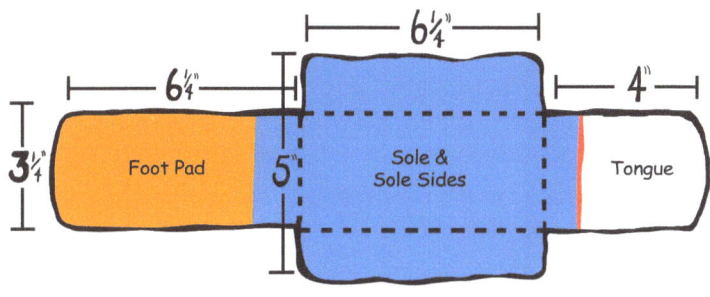

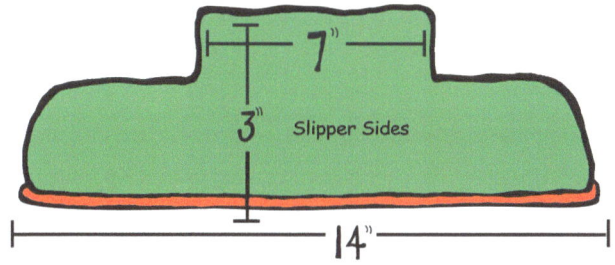

Finished size

Pattern is written for Sm/Junior size, with Toddler size appearing in parenthesis.

Sm/Junior: 6 ½" (4 ¾") toe to heel; 4 ½" (3 ¼") height; 3 ½" (2 ¾") width

Gauge

ESG Single Knitting:

4.25 sts (S) x 9.5 rows (R) per inch

ESG Double Knitting with ¾" spacing:

3.5 sts (S) x 4 rows (R) per inch

See Gauge and Size Calculators, Page 5

Needed

- Extra-small-gauge adjustable knitting board with at least 60 pegs to work as a panel, and with 20-peg pairs to work as double knitting: 12" ESG AJAL Knitting Board by Décor Accents Inc. used in sample.
- #4 Worsted Weight yarn in 3-5 colors- approx. 1/3rd skein (or less) of each: Vanna's Choice by Lion Brand in scarlet, fern, white, colonial blue and terracotta used in sample (black, scarlet and white used in toddler size); 100% acrylic, 170 yards per skein.
- Loom tool, crochet hook, tapestry needle, 2 stitch markers.
- Optional: cording for laces = 1 yard

Notes

Techniques used: U-Stitch/Flat Knit, Purl, Double Knit Stockinette, Panel Knitting, Half Hitch, Crochet CO, Basic BO, Increasing, Decreasing, Seaming.

This pattern uses one strand of yarn held throughout. All Knits and PFK are worked as U-Stitches/Flat Knits throughout.

Step by step

Set your loom to a board-knitting configuration to work in double knitting. SCO using footpad color (this will be the cushion on the inside of the slipper sole) onto 8 (5) peg pairs centered on the loom.

MAKIN' IT EASY!

Don't have a loom capable of double knitting? That's okay! For this portion of the project, the DK is used to make the footpad extra squishy. You can create the same effect by looming this portion double length and then folding in half during assembly. Or just make it as written, but using single knit, for a thinner footpad.

Sneaker Slippers, cont.

Row 1: DKS all pegs.

Rows 2-7 (2-4): Repeat the following 3-row pattern:

> **Row a:** Move peg pair loops from both ends to the outside of the knitting by one peg. Pull up the knitted loop from the previous row that is attached to the moved pegs onto the now empty pegs. DSK row.
>
> **Rows b & c:** DSK all pegs.

You will now have 12 (7) peg pairs filled on your loom.

Rows 8-26 (5-17): DKS all pegs.

Move back peg loops across to corresponding front pegs, so you will now have 2 loops on all front pegs, and none on the back.

You will now be switching from DK to PK on one side of the board only.

Row 27 (18): Using sole's outside color, K 2 loops over 1

Rows 28-36 (19-23): PFK all pegs.

Add Half Hitch loops to 3 pegs on each end of 12 (7) pegs being used for a total of 18 (13) pegs filled.

Rows 37-39 (24-42): K all pegs (toddler size proceed to * after Row 42)

Add 1 half hitch loop to each end of 18 pegs being used for a total of 20 pegs filled.

Rows 40-83: K all pegs.

Begin turning the toe area using the Short Row Method (Page 106) on all pegs, decreasing and W&T'ing until you have a total of 8 (4) pegs unwrapped. Increase back to 20 (13) pegs. Trim outside sole color, leaving a 30" tail for stitching shoe sides later.

Rows 84-89 (43-45): Using trim color, K all pegs.

Looking to the inside of your loom, pull up the knitted loops from Row 84 (43) back onto pegs and KO. Cut trim color, leaving a 20" tail for seaming.

Rows 90-130 (46-78): Using tongue color, K all, slipping 1st peg in each row.

Rows 131-137 (79-82): Knit in following 2-row pattern, decreasing one stitch each row until you have 12 (9) Sts remaining (adjust peg numbers/stitch counts to reflect decreases in repeat rows.):

> **Row a:** S1, D1, P16 (10), K1 (D1 = move 2nd loop from WY to 3rd peg & P 2 loops as one, move 1st

loop over 1 peg to fill gap.)

> **Row b:** S1, D1, K16 (10)

BBO remaining 12 (9) Sts.

Sole finishing

Complete your SCO of the footpad section. (Page 103)

Invisibly stitch heel corners together in a box shape, anchoring double knitted sole liner down in corners and invisibly across sole heel line. Continue anchoring entire liner inside sole at edges and toe.

Stitch top corners of turned toe down to sole edges to anchor closed. Weave in all ends, except long BO tail and trim colored tail, which will both be used for seaming.

Slipper sides

Using trim color, CCO 60 (50) pegs. Work as a flat panel.

Rows 1-6 (1-4): K all pegs.

Looking to the inside of your loom, pull up the knitted loops from Row 1 back onto pegs and KO.

Cut trim color yarn at 36" for seaming later on.

Rows 7-16 (5-10): Using slipper main color, PFK all pegs in following 2-row pattern:

> **Row a:** S1, K59 (49)
>
> **Row b:** S1, P2, K54 (44), P2, K1

Sneaker Slippers, cont.

Place stitch markers on pegs 15 (15) & 45 (35).

For the next 8 rows, you will be decreasing 1 peg at the start of each row, 4 pegs in from WY edge.

Work each dec. toward the center of your knitting.

Note: When you're making a dec. in a section that is surrounded by purls, make sure you purl your 2 loops together. On a section that is surrounded by knits, then you will make your dec. by knitting 2 loops together.

Row 17 (11): S1, K2, D1, K56 (46) = 59 (49) pegs remaining

Row 18 (12): S1, P2, D1, K52 (42), P2, K1 = 58 (48) pegs rem.

Row 19 (13): S1, K2, D1, K54 (44) = 57 (47) pegs rem.

Row 20 (14): S1, P2, D1, K50 (40), P2, K1 = 56 (46) pegs rem.

Row 21 (15): S1, K2, D1, K52 (42) = 55 (45) pegs rem.

Row 22 (16): S1, P2, D1, P10 (10), K28 (18), P12 (12), K1 = 54 (44) pegs rem.

Row 23 (17): S1, K2, D1, K50 (40) = 53 (43) pegs rem.

Row 24 (18): S1, P2, D1, P10 (8), K26 (16), P12 (10), K1 = 52 (42) pegs rem.

Row 25 (19): BBO to 1st stitch marker, K30 (20), BBO to end of row. Trim WY. You should now have 30 (20) pegs with loops.

Row 26 (20): Using new strand of slipper main color S1, P2, D1, K23 (13), P2, K1 = 29 (19) pegs rem.

Row 27 (21): S1, K2, D1, K25 (15) = 28 (18) pegs rem.

Row 28 (22): S1, P2, D1, K21 (11), P2, K1 = 27 (17) pegs rem. (Toddler size: proceed to * after Row 22 is worked)

Row 29: S1, K2, D1, K23 = 26 pegs rem.

Row 30: S1, P2, D1, K19, P2, K1 = 25 pegs rem.

*Row 31 (23): S1, K2, D1, K21 (13) = 24 (16) pegs rem.

Row 32 (24): S1, P2, D1, P19 (11), K1 = 23 (15) pegs rem.

Row 33 (25): S1, K2, D1, K19 (11) = 22 (14) pegs rem.

Row 34 (26): S1, P20 (12), K1 = 22 (14) pegs rem.

BBO all 22 (14) remaining pegs.

Weave in all ends except for long trim color tail.

Slipper sides finishing

Center the bottom edge of main slipper sides at back of sole section and pin evenly in place all around. Use trim-color tails to stitch sides securely in place to outermost edges of sole. Make sure that the sole sides and back are stitched so that they round upward to form a sort of cup, just right for a foot. Using the trim-colored tail left previously, stitch toe portions of shoe trim so that the trim at the toe section and the trim at the slipper sides overlap each other in a smooth, seamless line.

Add laces as you would thread normal shoe strings, using a tapestry needle to thread through the shoe top at the appropriate places. You can use a variety of items for this purpose; such as ribbon, I-Cord, purchased cording, crochet chains, etc.

You may add a circle, star, or other decorative items to the outside of each slipper. The sample uses a 1 ¼" crocheted circle.

Make a second one to complete your pair and enjoy your cool new Sneaker Slippers!

So Cool Cap

 EASY  MEDIUM  BULKY

This sporty and stylish hat is just the thing for any age, boy or girl! It can be worn pulled down over the ears for warmth, or up on the head in the style of a newsboy cap. The added ribbon trim makes the hat easily adjustable. Pair it with the Plush Baby Booties and you have an adorable set, perfect for gifting.

Finished sizes, gauges and materials

Newborn – 6 months (A):

- 15" circumference, 5" height from brim to crown, 6" total height including bill
- Fine Gauge (using U-St): 5.33 sts x 11 rows per inch (EvenKnit Sock Loom by Décor Accents Inc. used in sample)
- Worsted Weight yarn: approx. 2/3 skein (Red Heart Moon & Stars in pink chiffon used in sample, 52% acrylic, 48% nylon, 110 yards per skein)

6 months – Youth Small (B):

- 18" circumference, 7" height from brim to crown, 8.5" total height including bill
- Large Gauge (using U-St): 2.75 sts x 5.5 rows per inch (green round 36-peg Knifty Knitter loom used in sample)
- #5 Bulky Weight yarn: approx. 2/3 skein (Plymouth Yarn, Colorspun Chunky in #7124 used in sample, 75% acrylic, 26% wool, 143 yards per skein)

Youth-plus (C):

- 20" circumference, 8" height from brim to crown, 10" total height including bill
- Large Gauge (using EW): 2.66 sts x 4 rows per inch (purple round 48-peg Knifty Knitter hat loom used in sample)
- #5 Chunky Weight yarn: approx. 3/4 skein (Premier Yarns Deborah Norville Collection Serenity in Walden Pond used in sample, 100% acrylic, 109 yards per skein)

Needed

- Loom tool, crochet hook, tapestry needle, 3 stitch markers.
- Ribbon: 1 yard

Notes

Techniques used: U-Stitch, EW, Purl, Purl 2 Together, Crochet CO, Panel Knitting, Decreasing, Seaming.

This pattern uses one strand of yarn held throughout for all sizes.

The K's for sizes A and B are worked as U-Stitches, with C being worked as EW.

Step by step

Place stitch markers at pegs:

A: 19, 38 and 56.

B: 9, 18 and 27

C: 13, 25 and 37

Crochet CO in the round:

A: 74 pegs

B: 36 pegs

C: 48 pegs

*K1, P1 … Repeat from * to end of row for:

A: 6 rows

B & C: 5 rows

K all pegs for:

A: 34 rows (3")

B: 28 rows (5")

C: 18 rows (5.75")

Crown wedges

Working with only the first set of pegs before the first marker (A: pegs 1-18; B: pegs 1-8; C: 1-12), PK row.

*At the side with the WY, decrease one stitch (move the loop from 2nd peg to 3rd peg and KO, move the 1st peg's loop over one to fill gap).

PK row.*

Repeat between *'s until first section has no loops remaining.

So Cool Cap, cont.

Trim tail to 20" for seaming.

CO a new strand of WY and repeat procedure for the remaining 3 sections, until all pegs have been BO.

Using long tails, seam wedges invisibly together to form the crown.

Bill

Crochet CO 1/3 of the total pegs used for entire hat plus approx. one peg: (Leave a 20" CO tail for seaming later.)

A: 25 pegs

B: 13 pegs

C: 19 pegs

Place stitch markers at pegs:

A: 6, 13 and 20 (13 = center of bill; 6 and 20 = center of each side)

B: 4, 7 and 10 (7 = center of bill; 4 and 10 = center of each side)

C: 5, 10 and 15 (10 = center of bill; 5 and 15 = center of each side)

Row 1: S1, K remaining pegs

Row 2: Decrease at each marker. S1, Purl all except last peg which is Knit.

Note: All Decreases will be made with a P2tog, as they are nestled in a P row. Decrease the 2 outside markers by moving your loops in toward the center, making sure to move the markers to stay at the dec. stitch as you go. The center dec. will remain at the same peg each time, alternating which direction the dec. is made: first dec. row move loop to the right, next dec. row move loop to the left, but always to the same center marker.

Repeat this 2-row pattern until you are left with 1/3 of original CO number:

A: 8 pegs

B: 4 pegs

C: 6 pegs

BBO.

Pin bill to cap across short BO edge, including the sections on each side

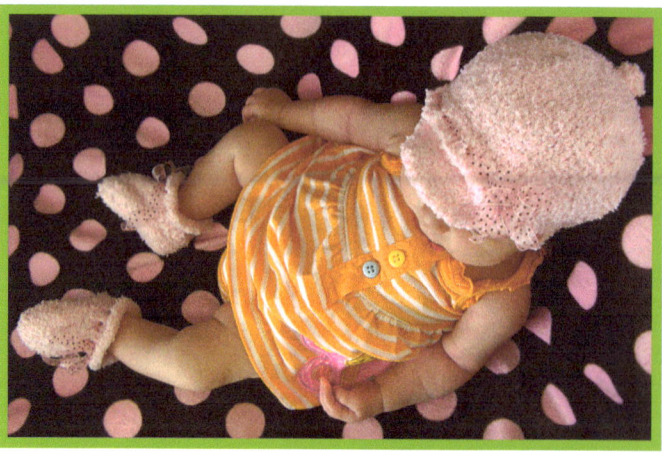

of the BO edge extending to each of the CO corners. This will help give your bill natural curve and support. The CO edge will be the outside edge of the bill. When pinning the bill, center the bill at the inside hat ribbing section, as well as with one crown panel. Using CO tail, stitch bill to hat.

The top-knot button is created by crocheting a 1" circle using single crochet stitch. Trim the tail at approx. 20" and apply a running stitch around the edge of the circle. The yarn ends are used as stuffing to fill the button. Gather using the running stitch to form a ball shape. Knot in place. The button is then stitched to the top of the hat, at the center where the wedges come together. If you prefer, a little pom-pom or a decorative button could be used in place of the crocheted button.

Weave in all ends and trim close to work.

Thread ribbon in and out of the ribbing stitches, centering horizontally.

The ribbon can be used to gather gently at the back of the hat for custom sizing, then worked into a pretty bow at one side of the bill. The ends can be curled with scissors just like curling ribbon for added cuteness!

For a more boyish look, you can use an appliqué patch over the ribbon, or fasten with a fun button or buckle.

Plush Baby Booties

EASY   MEDIUM

These comfy cozies are just the thing for toasty tootsies! With the looser ankle, they're easy to slip on baby's feet, but are not so likely to be kicked off once tied with the ribbon, which adds charm and adjustable comfort! Pick a nice plushy yarn for extra softness on baby's toes.

Finished size

Newborn - 3 months (3" from toe to heel, 6" ankle circumference when not gathered)

Gauge

5.33 sts (S) x 11 rows (R) per inch

See Gauge and Size Calculators, Page 5

Needed

- Fine-gauge loom with at least 32 pegs: EvenKnit Sock Loom by Décor Accents Inc. used in sample.
- **Worsted Weight yarn:** approx. 1/3 skein: Red Heart Moon & Stars in pink chiffon used in sample, 100% acrylic, 110 yards per skein.
- Loom tool, crochet hook, tapestry needle
- Ribbon: 1 yard in length x 3/8" width

Notes

Techniques used: U-Stitch, Purl, Crochet CO, Short Rows, Kitchener Stitch.

All K's are worked as U-Stitches throughout.

This pattern uses one strand of yarn throughout.

Step by step

Crochet CO 32 pegs to work in the round.

Rows 1-4: K all.

Rows 5-12: *K1, P1 ... Repeat from * to end of row.

Using Short Rows (Page 106), turn the heel using 16 pegs, decreasing down to 5 unwrapped pegs.

After the heel is complete, Knit 12 rows.

Turn the toe in exactly the same method as the heel.

Kitchener Stitch the toe seam (Page 109).

If more toe shaping is desired, apply a running stitch along the wrong-side of the toe seam to evenly cinch in just a bit.

Weave in all ends and trim close to work.

Thread ribbon in and out of the ankle ribbing stitches, centering it inside the 8 ribbed cuff rows.

Use the ribbon to gather the ankle area gently and then tie it into a pretty bow. The ends can be curled with scissors just like curling ribbon for added cuteness!

Pom-Pom Hat

BEGINNER — 6 SUPER BULKY

This adorable accessory will make any outing filled with fun! It's so simple to make and can be easily personalized to fit any child's style. Loomed with extra fluffy fiber, this hat's irresistible charm also lends itself perfectly to those heirloom photography sessions!

Finished size

This pattern is written for size Newborn-4 months.

15" circumference, 6.5" height (not including pom-poms)

Gauge

2.38 sts (S) x 3 rows (R) per inch

See Gauge and Size Calculators, Page 5

Needed

- Large-gauge loom with at least 33 pegs: yellow long 38-peg Knifty Knitter with loom clips used in sample.
- #6 Super Bulky Weight yarn: 1 skein: Sensations Sumptuous in blue/brown dot pattern used in sample; 100% acrylic, 62 yards per skein.
- Loom tool, crochet hook, tapestry needle, Pom-pom maker, sharp scissors.

Notes:

Techniques used: E-Wrap, Crochet CO, Basic BO, Seaming Double Knit BO, Pom-pom and Tassel Making.

This pattern uses one strand of yarn held throughout.

Step by step

Using your loom clips, adjust your loom to a 33-peg configuration. CCO all 33 pegs to work in the round:

Because this yarn is so bulky, this pattern employs a special EW technique. You will be wrapping every other peg, alternating pegs wrapped, each time around the loom. The benefit of using an odd number of pegs is that your wrapping will flow naturally into alternating the pegs wrapped for each row.

Rows 1-18 (6"): Work in the following 2-row pattern:

Row a: EW every odd number peg, beginning with peg 1 (keep the WY to the back of the pegs being skipped). KO.

Row b: EW every even-numbered peg, beginning with peg 2 (keep the WY to the back of the pegs beings skipped). KO.

BO all pegs, using the DKBO method. If you are using a round loom, then BBO all pegs, leaving enough tail for seaming. Press the BO edges flat together and seam.

Create 2 large pom-poms (following pom-pom maker's instructions) and attach them securely to each top corner of the hat.

Tassel Ties

Create two 2-peg I-Cords (Page 105) that are 7" in length. Leave approx. 20" long tail on both the CO and BO ends of the I-Cords for seaming and tassel making.

Using the CO tail, stitch the I-Cords to the bottom edge of the hat in line with the pom-poms.

See illustration on the left. Holding fingers together and straight, wrap a new length of WY around them 7 times. Trim.

Thread BO tail onto a yarn needle and then through all 7 loops and stitch them securely onto the end of the I-Cord Tie. Wrap BO tail a few times, tightly around the top portion of the loops, creating the top knot of the tassel. Knot to secure.

Hold all ends straight, including BO tail, and trim them evenly across. Fluff tassel to shape. Weave in all ends and trim close to work.

Steam block thoroughly to soften and mold. It helps to have something round and about 15-16" in circumference, to place your hat onto, so it will dry into the desired size and shape. A Styrofoam ball left in the plastic packaging works great for this!

Sweetheart Set

This set was originally created years ago, especially for my youngest daughter, whose birthday is just a day after Valentine's Day. She's always been my sweetheart girl, and this set was created just for her. How could anyone resist those sweet little I-Cord loops that add whimsy to both the hat's pom-pom and scarf? The mittens are an essential cold-weather item that any child can love.

Finished size

Hat: 8.75" in height (without pom-pom) by 8" wide, with a circumference of 17.5"; pom-pom measures approx. 3" in height by 4" in width.

Scarf: 54" in length by 3.5" in width, which will roll up on itself to about 1.5" across.

Mittens: Sample measures approx. 5.75" in length by 2.5" in width, thumb measures 1.75" in length by 1" in width.

Needed

▸ **LOOMS**

Hat & Scarf: Any large-gauge loom with at least 36 pegs: blue round 24-peg and green round 36-peg Knifty Knitter looms were used in sample.

Mittens: Any large-gauge adjustable loom with at least 14 pegs: pink long 26-peg Knifty Knitter and 2 loom clips were used in sample.

▸ **YARNS**

MC: Worsted Weight yarn: about 3 skeins: Lion Brand Wool-Ease in white multi used in sample; 78% acrylic, 19% wool, 3% polyester, 162 yards per skein.

CC: Worsted Weight yarn: about 2 skeins: Caron Jewel Box in ruby used in blanket sample; 64% acrylic, 20% rayon, 16% polyester, 100 yards per skein.

▸ Loom tool, crochet hook, tapestry needle, 2 stitch markers.

Notes

Techniques used: Popcorn Stitch, I-Cording, E-Wrap, U-Stitch, Purl, Decrease, Crochet CO, Basic BO, Drawstring BO.

The hat and scarf portion of this pattern uses two strands of MC yarn held throughout, except where the CC yarn is called for. When working with the CC, only one strand of yarn is held. The mitten portion of the pattern uses just one strand of MC when called for and just one strand of CC when called for.

In making the mittens, all Knit Stitches are worked as U-Stitches.

Hat

Step by step

Using one strand of CC, Crochet CO 36 pegs to work in the round.

*Rows 1-5: EW

Working on the inside of the loom and beginning at peg 2, count down 4 rows of the knitted piece. Grab the loop from the 4th row down and pull it up onto peg 2, above the base loop. Repeat this process with each even-numbered peg.

KO all pegs with 2 loops. This equals one row of Popcorn Stitch.

Repeat from * 2 more times for a total of 3 rows of Popcorn Stitch. Trim CC and set aside.

Holding 2 strands of MC together as one, EW all pegs in the round for 25 rows.

Gather BO. Without whip-stitching across the center hole, knot securely at the inside of the hat.

Pom-pom

Using one strand of CC, Crochet CO 24 pegs of a large-gauge loom to work in the round. (Loom options include: Knifty Knitter blue round 24-peg loom or pink long 26-peg loom with added loom clips, set at a 24-peg configuration.)

Rows 1-2: EW

Pegs 1 & 2: EW in I-Cord for 14 rows. This will be the first loop of your pom-pom.

Pegs 2 & 3: EW in I-Cord for 14 rows. This will be the second loop

Sweetheart Set, cont.

MAKIN' IT EASY!

The sample uses a type of chenille yarn for the CC. If you choose to use chenille when creating your own Sweetheart Set, make sure to remember to keep the tension loose while knitting with it. Chenille has zero elasticity and will easily break when it's pulled too tightly!

of your pom-pom.

Continue in this way, shifting over just one peg after each 14 row I-Cord loop until you have completed loops on the entire loom, ending with a last I-Cord loop worked on peg 24 and peg 1 to close the circle.

Reach inside the loom and pull the first row of stitches up onto the corresponding pegs. KO.

Gather BO. Cinch in tightly, just like in the top of the hat and tie yarn tails into a square knot. Pull these tails through the center hole at the top of the hat and securely stitch pom-pom in place. Weave in all ends.

Scarf

Notes

This scarf is meant to curl up into a tube, flaring the little loops out into fun frills. Because of this, there's no need to worry about slipping stitches on the edges — just EW throughout.

Step by step

Using one strand of CC, Crochet CO 10 pegs of a large-gauge loom. Work as a flat panel.

*Using the instructions for making the pom-pom, create a row of 9 I-Cord loops, using 12 rows for each loop, rather than 14.

Pull the first row of CC loop stitches up over the pegs. KO.

EW PK one row. Trim CC and set aside.

Using 2 strands of MC, EW PK 22 rows.

Repeat from * until you have 3 sections of CC I-Cord loops with 2 sections of MC in-between.

Using 2 strands of MC, EW PK 44 rows.

Continue the pattern again, until you have created an additional 3 sections of CC I-Cord loops with 22 rows of MC in-between each.

BBO all pegs. Weave in all ends.

Sweetheart Set, cont.

This project can be for both girls and boys. Simply leave off the decorative touches and you'll have a warm and cozy pair of mittens that any kid would love to snuggle their hands into.

Notes
In making the mittens, all Knit Stitches are worked as U-Stitches.

Gauge
3.25 sts (S) x 6 rows (R) per 1"

See Gauge and Size Calculators, Page 5

Perfect Fit Mitts (Make 2)

Step by step

Set your adjustable loom to 14 pegs (sample uses the pink long Knifty Knittor loom with added loom clips). Using one strand of CC, Crochet CO all pegs to work in the round.

Rows 1-10: *K1, P1, repeat from * to end of row.

Trim CC and set aside.

Row 11: Using 1 strand of MC, K all pegs in the round.

Rows 12-13: K all pegs, increasing one stitch each row at peg 1 for the left mitten and at peg 7 for the right mitten. Move clips and stitches as necessary. You will now have 16 pegs in use.

Rows 14-18: K all pegs.

Left Thumb: PFK, using only pegs 1-3, for 26 rows.

Right Thumb: PFK, using only pegs 7-9, for 26 rows.

Rows 19-28: K all pegs, working in the round again. Your thumb will be a loop with open sides that will be stitched up later.

Rows 29-36: Place a stitch marker at pegs 1 and 9. K all pegs, decreasing 1 stitch per row. Alternate ends of the loom you use to decrease each time; for example: Row 29: decrease at peg 1, Row 30: decrease at peg 9, Row 31: decrease at peg 1 and so on. Each time you create a decrease, move the stitch marker so that it stays at the decreased stitch while you move loops and loom clips in, as necessary.

Gather BO remaining 8 sts. Stitch thumb sides together invisibly and weave in all ends.

Bow embellishment

With a crochet hook, create a 5" chain, leaving an 8" tail on each end. Thread a tail onto yarn needle and pull through the center of cuff front, from the outside to the inside of the cuff, leaving all of the chain on the outside. Do the same with the other tail, just a stitch or 2 apart from the first. Tie these ends into a square knot.

Flatten the chain loop into a bow shape on the outside of cuff. Using your tails one at a time, stitch around the center of bow shape and back through cuff. Knot tails again at the inside. Weave in ends.

36 Loom Knitting for Little People

Jester Hat

 EASY  MEDIUM  BULKY

This is definitely a unique piece of headgear — both to wear and in the way the project is created. Have you ever played the game Tri-ominoes? The construction of this hat reminds me of placing all those triangles together to make shapes and designs. In this case, the hat is built out of triangles and mitered squares. This style is for those kids that love to be the life of the party everywhere they go!

Finished Size

18.5" circumference, 9.25" flat width, 7.5" in height at center diamond between two points.

To make this hat in a different size, increase or decrease the number of original CO pegs for both the mitered squares and the triangles. The number of pegs to CO for the triangles is 75% of the number used for the squares.

Gauge

3 sts x 5.75 rows per inch

Needed

- Large-gauge adjustable loom with at least 31 pegs: Sample uses yellow long 38-peg Knifty Knitter and loom clips.
- Purple Sample: #4 Worsted Weight yarn in 3 coordinating colors- approx. ¼ skein of each: Loops & Threads Impeccable in amethyst, dark forest and butterscotch used in sample; 100% acrylic, 277 yards per skein.
- Pink Sample: #5 Bulky Weight yarn in 5 coordinating colors- approx. ¼ - ½ skein of each: Lion Brand Baby's First in twinkle toes, cotton ball, sea sprite, honey bee, and beanstalk used in sample; 55% acrylic, 45% cotton, 120 yards per skein.
- Loom tool, crochet hook, tapestry needle

Notes

Techniques used: E-Wrap, Purl, Panel Knit, CCO, Basic BO, Decreasing, K2Tog, P2Tog, Picking Up Sts, Seaming.

This pattern uses one strand of yarn held throughout when using #5 bulky weight yarn (as in pink sample) and 2 strands held throughout when using #4 worsted weight yarn (as in purple sample).

All Knits are worked as E-Wraps throughout pattern.

Making a mitered square

This is a fun process that works almost like magic! You will be starting with the number of stitches that are needed to form two adjoining sides of your square. The square shape happens when you decrease two stitches at the center peg every other row; in this case, each purl row. When you make your decreases, you will first be moving the loop to the left of the center peg over to and above the loop on the center peg. The loop to the right of the center peg will then be moved over to and above the loop on the center peg. Adjust the loom clip to close in the gaps as you decrease.

Once you have moved your loops to the center peg, you'll work those three loops together as one, as you purl the row. If you'd like a bumpy look to the line going down the center of the hat (as in the purple sample), then you will purl those three loops together. If you like the look of a chain running down the center of the hat (as in the pink sample), then you will knit those three loops together.

Step by step

Place a loom clip so that it is at one end of your loom. You will be casting on so that the middle stitch of the total number of stitches being used is at the loom clip peg.

Using the color that will be the front diamond of the hat, CCO 31 pegs, from right to left, with the loops positioned as stated above. When using 31 pegs, the loom clip should mark your 16th peg. Work as a flat panel.

Jester Hat, cont.

Rows 1-31: Panel knit in the following 2-row pattern:

Row a: EW all pegs. (left to right)

Row b: P all pegs, working a decrease at the loom clip peg. (right to left)

Repeat Row a and Row b until there is just one loop left. BO last loop. Trim WY.

Square 2

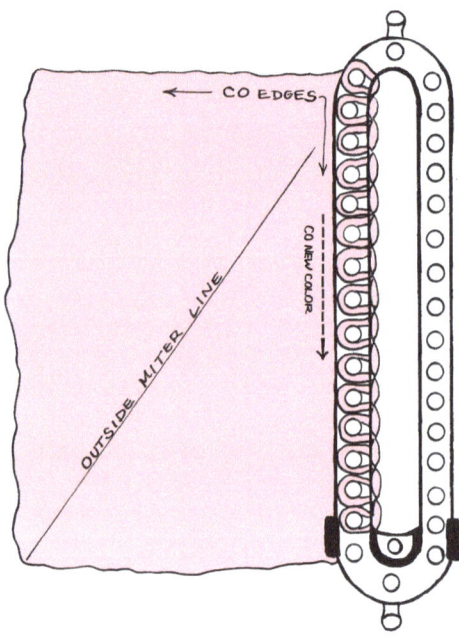

Using the diagram for reference, pick up the stitches from the previous square and place them back onto the loom as shown.

Using the color that will be the point of the hat on the left side, and leaving a 20" tail for seaming, EW 31 pegs from left to right, centering the loops at the loom clips. The last 15 pegs will be empty, so your EW's will be the CO row for these pegs.

Work this next square in exactly the same method as before. Treat your CO row as your first EW row. You will be knitting the left side point of the hat.

When 3 pegs are remaining, work as a 3-peg I-Cord for 2". D1 to continue with a 2 peg I-Cord for 1 ½". D1 to just one peg remaining and EW 5 chains.

BO last loop. Trim WY.

Square 3

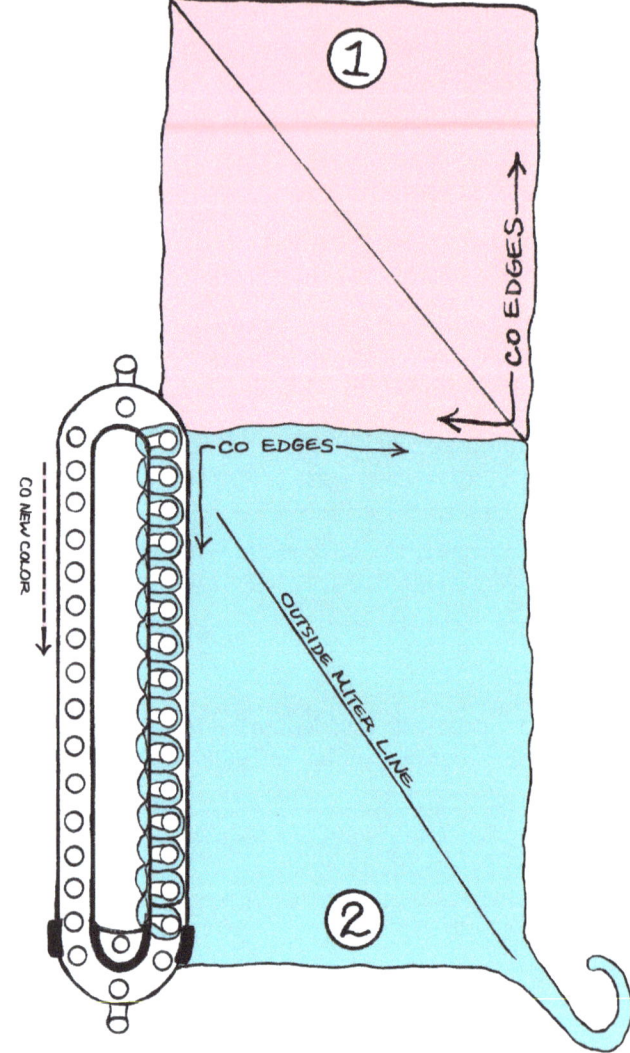

Using the diagram for reference, pick up the stitches from the previous square and place them back onto the loom as shown.

Using the color that will be the back triangle of the hat, EW 31 pegs, from left to right, centering the loops at the loom clips. Pegs 1-16 will be empty, so your EW's will be the CO row for these pegs.

Work this next square in exactly the same method as in the first square. Treat your CO row as your first EW row. You will be knitting the back center of the hat.

Jester Hat, cont.

Square 4

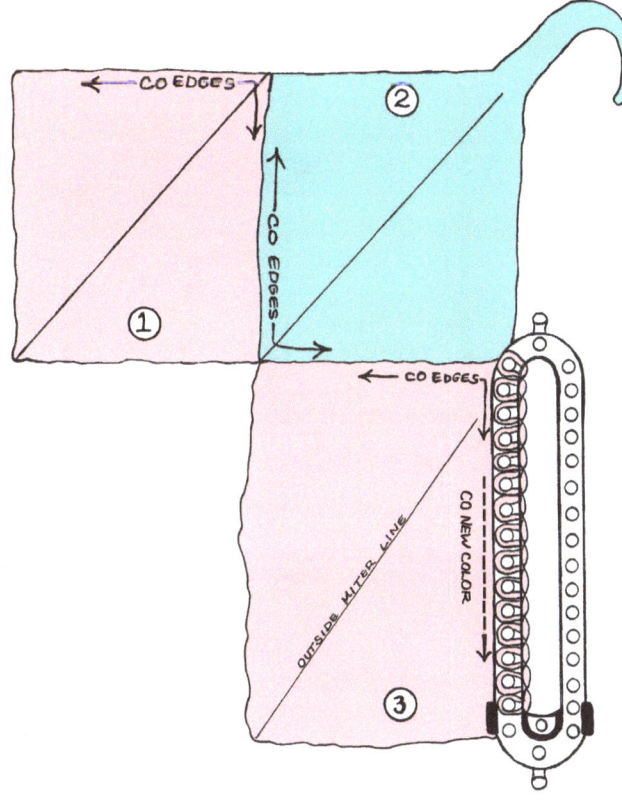

Using the diagram for reference, pick up the stitches from the previous square and place them back onto the loom as shown.

Using the color that will be the point of the hat on the right side, and leaving a 20" tail for seaming, EW 31 pegs, from left to right, centering the loops at the loom clips. The last 15 pegs will be empty, so your EW's will be the CO row for these pegs.

Work this next square in exactly the same method as directed for square #2. Treat your CO row as your first EW row. You will be knitting the right side point of the hat.

Triangles

Using the color that will be the lower left side of the hat, CCO 23 pegs. Work as a flat panel.

Rows 1-23: Repeat the following 2-row pattern:

Row a: P all pegs. After row is worked, make a dec. 3 pegs in from both outside edges (move the loop from the 3rd peg from each end over to the 2nd peg from each end).

Row b: EW all pegs. K2tog at the pegs with 2 loops from the dec in Row a. Move the sts in to close the gaps.

When there is only one peg remaining, trim the WY to 30" for seaming. Pull WY through the loop and cinch.

Repeat the triangle instructions to create the lower right side of the hat.

Using the long BO tails, stitch the two triangles into place in the lower corners of the hat to form the brim area. Stitch the front square at the open side together with the right side point's lower edge. Lastly, stitch the two top point edges together. Make sure these are not stitched too tightly, so that the points still want to droop outward.

Weave in all ends and trim close to work.

Tie an overhand knot into each of the points. Fold up the bottom edge for a brim.

Steam block thoroughly to soften and mold. It helps to have something round and about 18-20" in circumference, to place your hat onto, so it will dry into the desired size and shape. A Styrofoam ball left in the plastic packaging works great for this.

Pair with the Silly Sidewinder or the Crazy Caterpillar for a perfectly kooky matched set!

Felted Fun Hat

 MODERATE  BULKY 5  MEDIUM 4

They say that laughter heals the soul. I think just looking at a hat as fun and wacky as this one lifts the spirits and puts a bounce in the step of all who see it. Imagine how it feels to actually wear it! It's a perfect party or costume accessory for kids of all ages — from 5 to 105 years young!

Finished size

22" head opening circumference; 9" total height; 2.5" brim width; 8.5" across top; 12" total width

You can create this hat in other sizes, simply by changing up the way your yarn is used. A hat made with the same instructions, but using 2 strands of worsted weight throughout, resulted in a head circumference of 19.75" and height of 7.5".

Gauge

2.25 sts (S) x 3.33 rows (R) per inch (before felting)

See Gauge and Size Calculators, Page 5

Needed

- Large-gauge loom with at least 36 pegs: 36-peg green round Knifty Knitter used in sample.
- **#5 Bulky Weight yarn:** approx. 220 yards each of 3 coordinating colors.

  Sample uses: Knit Picks Cadena in Neptune (MC1) & in blackberry (MC2); 70% wool, 30% superfine alpaca, 110 yards per skein. To give the hat a bit of pizzazz, 1 skein of #4 Worsted Weight (using 3 strands as one) was also used in sample: Lion Brand Felting Wool in goldenrod (CC); 100% wool, 158 yards.
- Loom tool, 6.5 mm crochet hook, tapestry needle, knitting marking pins, hot water/washing machine, laundry bag, and 1 tbsp laundry soap for felting.
- Optional: If you need to create a head insert for better fit, you'll also need: a craft handkerchief, duct tape, hot glue, and four 3" pieces of adhesive Velcro.

Notes

Techniques used: E-Wrap, Panel Knit, Short Rows, Crochet CO, Basic BO, Seaming, Felting.

This pattern uses two strands of yarn held throughout, except when working with the worsted weight yarn, which is worked with three strands of yarn held together as one.

MAKIN' IT EASY!

You will be creating sections of short row wedges, alternating colors with each wedge. When switching colors, there's no need to trim your WY. Just be sure to pull the new color to be used up and over the top of all the resting colors.

Step by step

Pinwheel top

Using one of the 3 colors, CCO 14 pegs in a left to right direction.

To make a short-row wedge:

You will be working these as a flat panel, beginning with just 2 pegs and increasing by one peg every two rows. This is how they're worked:

*Rows 1 & 2: S1, K1.

Rows 3 & 4: S1, K2.

Rows 5 & 6: S1, K3.

Rows 7 & 8: S1, K4.

Rows 9 & 10: S1, K5.

Rows 11-27: continue in this same manner, knitting one additional peg per 2 rows.

Row 28: Drop color (do not cut!) and CO the next color. (see Makin' it Easy tip) Work the row: S1, K13.

After Row 28, you should be back at the 1st peg and with all 14 pegs having been worked with short rows. You are ready to

Felted Fun Hat, cont.

continue to the next wedge, with the new color of yarn you've just switched to.

Repeat from * for a total of 6 wedges, alternating one of the 3 colors for each wedge.

At the end of the 6th wedge, BBO all pegs, leaving a long enough tail for seaming. Stitch the circle closed at the sides and at the center of the circle. Weave in all ends and trim close to work.

Striped sides

Using your MC1 (sample uses neptune), CCO 36 pegs. Work as a flat panel.

Work in the following pattern:

Rows 1-8: MC1- EW all pegs.

Rows 9 & 10: CC (sample uses goldenrod)- EW all pegs.

Rows 11-18: MC2 (sample uses blackberry)- EW all pegs.

Rows 19 & 20: CC- EW all pegs.

Rows 21-28: MC1- EW all pegs.

Rows 29 & 30: CC- EW all pegs.

Rows 31-38: MC2- EW all pegs.

BBO all pegs, leaving a long enough tail for seaming.

Make a total of two side panels, following the instructions above for each panel.

Short-row brim

Using one of the 3 colors, CCO 8 pegs in a left to right direction.

You will be working these as a flat panel, with partial short rows for gradual shaping around the brim. This is how they're worked:

*Rows 1 & 2: EW8.

Row 3: EW6. After working the 6th peg, pull one of the two strands from the 7th peg over onto the 6th peg. Knit this extra loop into the first stitch of the next row. This will help fill in the gap caused by the short rows.

Row 4: EW6.

Rows 5-18: Repeat from * making sure to end with 2 full 8-peg rows.

CO a new color and repeat these 18 rows. You will have a total of 9 color wedges, alternating 1 of the 3 colors for each wedge.

At the end of the 9th wedge, BBO all pegs, leaving a long enough tail for seaming onto hat sides. Weave in all ends and trim close to work.

Assembly

Using your BO tails, seam the 2 side panels together at each of the sides so that they create a tube shape. Make sure stripes line up.

Using your knitting marking pins, attach the Pinwheel Top onto the top edge of the Striped Sides tube, keeping any extra spacing evenly dispersed around the entire top. Stitch in place.

Pin the brim around the outside of the bottom section of the striped sides tube, keeping even throughout. Make sure you are pinning the brim so that it is attached sticking out from the sides at a right angle, rather than hanging downward from the bottom edge. Stitch evenly in place.

Weave in any yarn tails and trim close to work.

Felted Fun Hat, cont.

Finishing

Felt your project as listed on Page 111.

Find something that is just the right shape and circumference to let your hat dry in the desired form. I used a plastic canister that just happened to be a perfect fit. Make sure to keep checking the hat's progress as it dries to keep shaping and molding during the setting process.

If you feel you need a little extra head support for a better fit, or more comfortable wearing, you can make your own customized head liner. Just follow these instructions:

Drape a craft handkerchief around the head of the person who is to wear the hat, or around a head form.

Wrap duct tape lightly around the widest portion of the head, over the top of the handkerchief.

Once around the circumference should be just fine. Remove from the person's head or head form.

Fold the extra edges of fabric over twice, so that it covers up the duct tape and so that the outside edges of the handkerchief are tucked inside the folds. Hot glue or stitch these folds in place.

Place the liner back onto the person's head or on the head form.

Using both sides of the 4 strips of adhesive Velcro, with only one side's tape cover removed, stick evenly in place around base of the head liner and press firmly.

Remove the other side's tape cover and carefully place the felted hat on the person's head, down over the head liner.

Press at each of the 4 places with Velcro to firmly adhere. Let adhesive set as per package instructions before trying to separate Velcro.

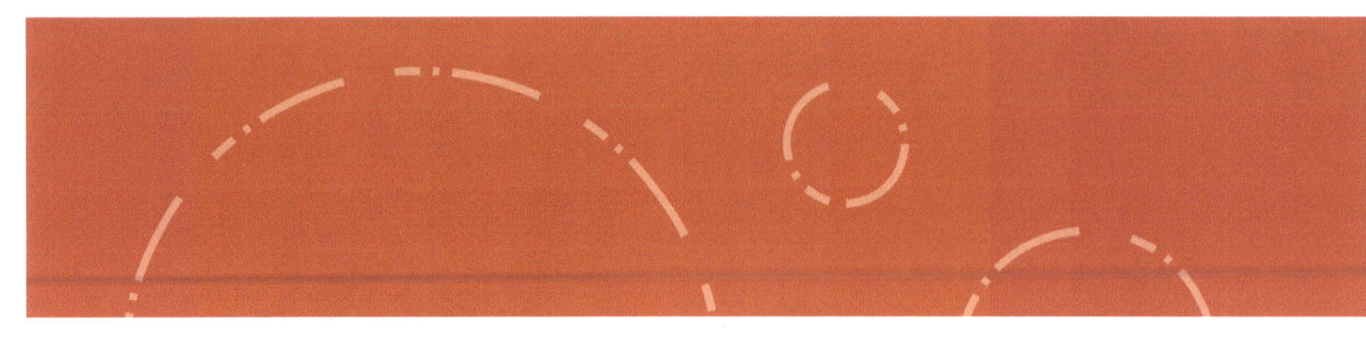
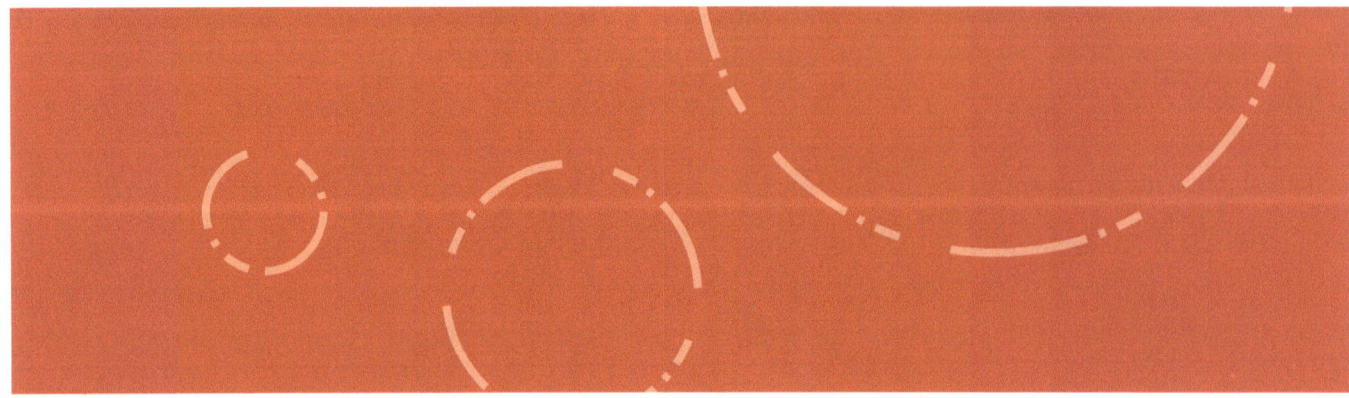

Sporty Visor

EASY — 4 MEDIUM

What a fun and spunky little item to keep the sun out of your children's eyes, and help them stay cool and stylin'! Personalize it with school or favorite sports colors to show some team spirit!

Finished size, gauges and materials

Newborn – Toddler (A):

- 16" circumference, 2" height from brim to crown, 1.75" bill

- **Extra-small-gauge (using EW):** 4.5 sts x 10 rows per inch (Extra-small-gauge adjustable loom by Décor Accents Inc. with at least 28 pegs used in sample)

- **Worsted Weight yarn:** approx. 1/3 skein (Vanna's Choice by Lion Brand in scarlet used in sample, 100% acrylic, 170 yards per skein). A very small amount of the same yarn in a coordinating color is used for the decorative stitching on the strap.

Youth (B):

- 20" circumference, 2" height from brim to crown, 2" bill

- **Extra-small-gauge (using EW):** 4.5 sts x 10 rows per inch (Extra-small-gauge adjustable loom by Décor Accents Inc. with at least 28 pegs used in sample)

- **Worsted Weight yarn:** approx. ¼ skein (Red Heart Super Saver in camouflage used in sample, 100% acrylic, 146 yards per skein)

Additional items needed

- Loom tool, crochet hook, tapestry needle, 3 stitch markers
- 2 decorative buttons

Notes

Techniques used: EW, Purl, Purl 2 Together, Crochet CO, Panel Knitting, Half Hitch, Decreasing, Seaming.

This pattern uses one strand of yarn held throughout for both sizes.

Step by step

Headband

Figure the desired circumference you'll need for your visor headband by measuring your child's head and subtracting 1" for a better fit. We will be working this measurement in thirds.

Crochet CO 9 pegs.

*****Row 1:** S1, EW8

Row 2: S1, P7, EW1

Repeat from * until you've reached 1/3rd of your required measurement.

Next section of thirds:

Set-up row: S1, EW8, Half Hitch 2 (for 2 additional pegs) (Page 101).

*****Row 1:** S1, P9, EW1

Row 2: S1, EW10

Repeat from * until you've reached 2/3 of your required measurement, ending after Row 1.

Last section of thirds:

Set-up row 1: BBO 2 pegs, S1, P7, EW1

*****Row 1:** S1, EW8

Row 2: S1, P7, EW1

Repeat from * on original 9 pegs until you've reached your final required headband measurement.

Graft the live loops from the 9 pegs end to end with the CO end. You can use the Kitchener Stitch for this, or invisibly hand stitch together so there is no interruption of the garter stitch.

Fold the extra width from the center third up onto the right side of the headband so that the fold is even with the rest of the headband edge and stitch into place.

Sporty visor, cont.

Bill

Crochet CO ⅓ of the total pegs used for headband plus approx. one peg: (Leave a 20" CO tail for seaming later.)

Size A: 23 pegs

Size B: 28 pegs

Place stitch markers at pegs:

Size A: 6, 12 and 18 (12 = center of bill; 6 and 18 = center of each side)

Size B: 7, 14 and 21 (14 = center of bill; 7 and 21 = center of each side)

Row 1: S1, K remaining pegs

Row 2: Decrease at each marker. S1, Purl all except last peg which is Knit.

Note: *All Decreases will be made with a P2tog, as they are nestled in a P row. Decrease the 2 outside markers by moving your loops in toward the center, making sure to move the markers to stay at the dec. stitch as you go. The center dec. will remain at the same peg each time, alternating which direction the dec. is made: first dec. row move loop to the right, next dec. row move loop to the left, but always to the same center marker.*

Repeat this 2-row pattern until you are left with ⅓ of original CO number:

A: 8 pegs

B: 10 pegs

BBO, keeping a 20" tail.

Pin bill to headband across short BO edge, including

the sections on each side of the BO edge extending to each of the CO corners. The CO edge will be the outside edge of the bill. When pinning the bill, center it under the turned up portion at the front of the headband, keeping edges even. Using CO tail stitch securely in place, working the bill upward with your stitches, toward the folded section, to help give the bill more structure.

Weave in all ends and trim close to project.

Using a contrasting yarn, add blanket stitching around the outside edge of the folded area to make it look like a strap. Decorative buttons can then be stitched securely in place at each outside edge. You can personalize your visors to match each child's personality. Just have fun with it!

accessories

Pacifier Pals

EASY MEDIUM SUPER BULKY

When my girls were babies, one of the things that was a constant pull on my attention was keeping those pacifiers clean and off the floor, especially once they learned the "let's see how many times mom picks this up after I throw it down" game. These Pacifier Pals give moms the winning edge, while also looking so fun and adorable perched on a little one's collar. These little guys help make happy babies — and definitely happy moms!

Binky Blossom

Finished size

4" total width and height; pacifier strap is 7.5" in length.

Gauge

3 sts (S) x 8 rows (R) per inch

See Gauge and Size Calculators, Page 5

Needed

- Large-gauge loom with at least 25 pegs: Sample uses 26-peg pink long Knifty Knitter and loom clips.
- #4 Worsted Weight yarn in 3 coordinating colors — a very small amount used of each: Loops & Threads Impeccable in dark pink, turquoise, and fern used in sample; 100% acrylic, 277 yards per skein. Just a tiny bit of Loops & Threads Impeccable in butterscotch and black was also used in creating the face.
- Wooden circle (sample uses 1¾" circles by Lara's Crafts)
- Your choice of findings to create the clip portion of the Pacifier Pal. (See Makin' it Easy! tip for ideas.)
- Loom tool, crochet hook, tapestry needle

Notes

Techniques used: U-Stitch, Purl, Panel Knit, Drawstring CO, Gather BO Basic BO, I-Cording, Seaming.

This pattern uses one strand of yarn held throughout. All Knits are worked as U-Stitches throughout pattern.

Step by step

Head instructions for all 3 Pacifier Pals:

Set your loom and clips to a 6 peg configuration. Using the head color for the clip you are creating (blossom, bear, or ducky), DSCO 6 pegs to work in the round.

Binky Blossom and Just Ducky

Rows 1-14: K all pegs.

Bear Buddy

Rows 1-8: K all pegs.

All Three

Gather BO all pegs. Knot securely, leaving a long enough yarn tail to use as stuffing inside the head piece.

Insert wooden circle flat on top of your yarn stuffing. If you find that you can see the wood through the knitting, remove the circle and wrap it completely with the same colored yarn you've used for your head color. You may now re-insert it on top of the yarn tail stuffing.

Pull on CO tail to cinch opening tightly closed. Knot securely, leaving a 16" long tail for stitching clip to back of head piece during assembly.

Petals

Set your loom and clips to a 25-peg configuration. Using the petal colored yarn, DSCO 25 pegs to work in the round. Leave a 10" CO tail for seaming.

*Rows 1-10: Working only on pegs 1-5, panel knit in the following 2-row pattern:

> **Row a:** S1, K4
>
> **Row b:** S1, P3, K1

BBO pegs 1-5. Trim WY.

Repeat from * on the next 5 pegs in line, until you have created a total of 5 individual petals.

49

Pacifier Pals, cont.

Pull on the CO tail until your petals shape around your flower head in just the way you like. Stitch them into place using the CO tail and tapestry needle.

Create the flower's pom-pom nose by tying 4-5 small lengths of nose-colored yarn into tight knots at the nose area. Use a tapestry needle to unravel the yarn plies. Rub ends between your fingers to fluff. Trim into desired shape.

Using a small bit of black yarn, embroider the eyes and mouth features as desired around the nose.

Pacifier strap/stem

You may use your pre-made pacifier clip to stitch into place at the back of the head, or create your own strap using the following instructions:

Create an 8" I-Cord using 3 pegs of your loom. Leave 12" long yarn tails at both ends for assembly.

Using the I-Cord yarn tails, tightly secure the I-Cord/Stem at one end to the clothing clip, and at the other end to the lobster clip.

Using the CO tail at the head piece, tightly secure the clothing clip to the back side of the head. Make sure the head is stitched on in an upright direction, with the clip's pincher end also facing up to easily grab a collar.

Weave in all ends and trim close to work.

MAKIN' IT EASY!

There are a few different options available for assembling your Pacifier Pal into clips. You can purchase a pre-made pacifier clip found in the baby section of most department stores (Bear sample uses MAM Fashion Pacifier Keeper. Duck sample uses the extra ribbon in the MAM package.) Or you can make your own clips by using findings available in your craft store's beading department (Duck and Blossom sample use Badge Clip with swivel by Beadalon, Lobster Clasps by Hirschberg Schutz & Co. Both of these measure 1¼" long x ½" wide). Just make sure you are aware of the child safety precautions for any findings you use in your design.

Pacifier Pals, cont.

Just Ducky

Finished Size
2.25" wide, 2.5" in height, pacifier strap is 8.25" in length.

Gauge
3 sts (S) x 8 rows (R) per inch

See Gauge and Size Calculators, Page 5

Needed
- Large-gauge loom with at least 10 pegs: Sample uses pink long 26-peg Knifty Knitter and loom clips.
- #4 Worsted Weight yarn in 2 coordinating colors — a very small portion used of each: Loops & Threads Impeccable in butterscotch and rouge used in sample; 100% acrylic, 277 yards per skein. Just a tiny bit of Loops & Threads Impeccable in black was also used in creating the face.
- Wooden circle (sample uses 1 ¾" circles by Lara's Crafts)
- Your choice of findings to create the clip portion of the Pacifier Pal. (See Makin' it Easy! tip for ideas.)
- Loom tool, crochet hook, tapestry needle, tiny bit of white fabric paint.

Notes
Techniques used: U-Stitch, Purl, Panel Knit, Drawstring CO, Crochet CO, Gather BO Basic BO, I-Cording, Seaming.

This pattern uses one strand of yarn held throughout.

All Knits are worked as U-Stitches throughout pattern.

Step by step
Follow the Head Instructions for all 3 Pacifier Pals, found in the Binky Blossom pattern.

Beak
Using your beak colored yarn, CCO 5 pegs. Work as a flat panel.

Rows 1-14: Work in the following 2-row pattern:

> **Row a:** S1, K4
>
> **Row b:** S1, P3, K1

Row 15: BBO peg 1, K3

Row 16: BBO peg 1, P1, K1

Row 17: S1, K2

Row 18: S1, P1, K1

BBO all 3 pegs. Trim WY, leaving a 12" BO tail for seaming.

Using the BO tail, stitch the beak to the head so that the wider end is on the top and is longer than the narrower end. Whipstitch the 2 sides together just a bit to form a beak shape.

Embroider the eyes using a bit of black yarn. A little dot of white fabric paint added to the upper corners of the left or right side of the eyes gives your ducky a lifelike sparkle.

Make sure to add the dot to the same side of the each eye (left or right) so he won't end up looking cross-eyed.

To create the head fluff, thread small lengths of beak-colored yarn through the top of the head and tie together randomly. Use your tapestry needle to unravel the plies in the yarn to create his frizzy fluff.

Using the CO tail at the back of the ducky's head, stitch either a pre-made clip in place, or use your own 8" I-Cord, as described in the Binky Blossom instructions.

Weave in all ends and trim close to work.

Pacifier Pals, cont.

Bear Buddy

Finished size
4" at widest point, 2.5" in height; pacifier strap is 7.5" in length

Gauge
2.5 sts (S) x 6 rows (R) per inch on average.

See Gauge and Size Calculators, Page 5

Needed
- Large-gauge loom with at least 10 pegs: Sample uses pink long 26-peg Knifty Knitter and loom clips.
- #6 Super Bulky Weight yarn for Head: a small amount of Patons Allure in mink used in sample; 100% nylon, 47 yards per skein.
- #4 Worsted Weight yarn for Face in 2 colors — a very small amount of each: Vanna's Choice by Lion Brand in scarlet and denim mist used in sample; 100% acrylic, 170 yards per skein.
- Wooden circle (sample uses 1¾" circles by Lara's Crafts)
- Your choice of findings to create the clip portion of the Pacifier Pal. (See Makin' it Easy! tip for ideas.)
- Loom tool, crochet hook, tapestry needle, tiny bit of white fabric paint.

Notes
Techniques used: U-Stitch, EW, Purl, Panel Knit, Drawstring CO, Crochet CO, Gather BO Basic BO, I-Cording, Seaming.

This pattern uses one strand of yarn held throughout.

All Knits are worked as U-Stitches throughout pattern.

Step by step
Follow the Head Instructions for all 3 Pacifier Pals, found in the Binky Blossom pattern.

Ears
Using your head/ear-colored yarn, EWCO 5 pegs. Work as a flat panel.

Rows 1-4: Work in the following 2-row pattern:

    Row a: S1, P3, EW1

    Row b: S1, EW4

Row 5: S1, P3, EW1

Gather BO all pegs tightly. Knot and use yarn tail to stitch BO edge to head.

Repeat from * to make a second ear.

Muzzle
Note: The bear's muzzle and face are created using many of the same techniques as were used for Koby the Striped Kitty, just on a smaller scale. (Details found on Page 80.)

Set your loom and clips to an 8-peg configuration. Using the muzzle yarn color, DSCO 8 pegs to work in the round. Leave a 25" long tail for seaming later.

Rows 1-6: K all pegs.

Gather BO all pegs, leaving a long enough yarn tail for use as stuffing inside the muzzle piece.

Pacifier Pals, cont.

Pull BO tail tight and knot securely. Stuff muzzle piece with BO tail. The DSCO tail can then be pulled just a tiny bit to form the cupped edge that will be sewn against the bear's head.

Using a tapestry needle threaded with the CO tail, whipstitch the mouth line by sewing through the center hole and around one side of the muzzle. Cinch tightly and knot to secure.

Still using CO tail, stitch the muzzle in place onto the bear's face. Carry the tail up through the inside of the face and out through the center of one of the ears. Embroider a small patch for the inside ear accent. Do the same for the other ear.

Using the accent colored yarn, embroider the bear's nose and eyes. If desired, a little dot of white fabric paint can be added to the upper corners of the left or right side of the eyes, as detailed in the ducky clip.

Using the CO tail at the back of the bear's head, stitch either a pre-made clip in place, or use your own 8" I-Cord, as described in the Binky Blossom instructions.

Weave in all ends and trim close to work.

MAKIN' IT EASY!

You can easily convert the Buddy Bear pattern into a puppy just by changing out the ear styles! All you have to do is add 2 additional rows to the ear instructions, keeping to the 2-row repeated pattern. Stitch the longer ears in place on the head leaving in a floppy, puppy shape. With a little experimenting, he could easily be made into a cat or a mouse too!

54 Loom Knitting for Little People

Rwanda Wristers & Walkabout Bag

EASY — SUPER BULKY 6

This fun set — full of texture and rugged usability for all those day-trip adventures — has been created with an additional purpose in mind. The yarn used in these projects comes from a wonderful organization called KidKnits, which was founded by a 9-year-old girl to help spread the love of crafting and to nurture the idea that "you're never too young to change a life on the other side of the world." — Ellie, Founder of KidKnits.org.

KidKnits specializes in selling craft kits which include a green 36-peg knitting loom, loom tool, yarn needle; and a skein of hand spun merino wool yarn. The yarn is dyed with indigenous ingredients by widows in Rwanda, earning a living for their families. All of these items are packaged stylishly in a handcrafted project bag that also helps raise funds to meet the needs of these ladies.

You can create the two projects featured here with four skeins of the KidKnits yarn: one ball of each of the four naturally vibrant colors. What a great way to use the art of looming to help people in need around the world!

Needed

- Large-gauge loom with at least 36 pegs: 36-peg green round Knifty Knitter loom was used in sample.
- #6 Super Bulky Weight yarn in 4 colors, approx. 1 skein each of KidKnits Yarn in indabo, ikigina, inturusu, and umweru used in sample; 100% wool, 70 yards per skein.
- Loom tool, crochet hook, tapestry needle, knitting marking pins, 1" decorative button.

Gauge

2.5 sts (S) x 4.75 rows (R) per inch

See Gauge and Size Calculators, Page 5

Notes

Techniques used: U-Stitch, Purl, Panel Knitting, Crochet CO, Basic BO, Decreasing, Knit 2 Together, Purl 2 Together, Seaming Blanket Stitch.

These patterns use one strand of yarn held throughout.

All Knits are worked as U-Stitches throughout.

Rwanda Wristers

Finished size

Junior size: 8" circumference, 4.75" in height

Step by step

Using just one color of your four yarns, CCO 13 pegs. Work as a flat panel.

Rwanda Wristers & Walkabout Bag, cont.

Rows 1-36: You will be repeating the same 3-row pattern throughout. Each time Row c is completed, trim WY and change to the next color in your four-color pattern:

>**Row a:** S1, K12
>
>**Row b:** S1, P11, K1
>
>**Row c:** S1, K12

BBO all pegs. Leave a 20" tail for seaming.

Weave in all ends and trim close to work.

Make another wrister, keeping the stripes identical.

Finishing

Using long yarn tail, seam CO and BO edges together leaving a 1¼"-1½" opening for thumb.

Crochet two 10" chains (sample uses the same color as is used for the Front Closure Strap on the Walkabout Bag) and weave one through the purl bumps across the wrist areas of each wrister. Tie an overhand knot in the chain at the outside of the wrist. Lightly block, stretching wristers in shape as they dry.

Walkabout Bag

Finished size

Bag: 9" in width, 7.25" in height, 2.75" deep.

Strap: 24" in length, 12" carrying height, 2.75" wide.

Step by step

Sides and strap

Using just one color of your four yarns, CCO 36 pegs. Work as a flat panel.

*Rows 1-12: You will be repeating the same 3-row pattern throughout. Each time Row c is completed, trim WY and change to the next color in your four color pattern:

>**Row a:** S1, K35
>
>**Row b:** S1, P34, K1
>
>**Row c:** S1, K35

BBO all pegs. Leave a 12" tail for seaming.

Repeat from * to create a total of three, 4-color striped panels, each measuring 16" long. Make sure to keep the stripes identical in each panel.

Using BO tails, stitch these panels invisibly together end to end to create a continuous panel that is now 48" in circumference.

Weave in all ends and trim close to work.

Front panel

Using just one color of your four yarns, CCO 24 pegs. Work as a flat panel.

Rows 1-27: S1, K23

Row 28: S1, P22, K1

Row 29: S1, K23

Row 30: S1, P22, K1

BBO all pegs.

Back panel and flap

Using a different colored yarn of your four than the one you used for your Front Panel, CCO 24 pegs. Work as a flat panel.

Rwanda Wristers & Walkabout Bag, cont.

Rows 1-27: S1, K23

Row 28: S1, P22, K1

Row 29: S1, K23

Row 30: S1, P22, K1. Cut WY.

Rows 31-54: Add the color you'd like for your flap and work in the following 2-row pattern:

> **Row a:** S1, K23
>
> **Row b:** S1, P2, K18, P2, K1

Rows 55-64: Work in the same 2-row pattern, but D1 st on the 4th peg in from the WY on each row (move the loop from peg 4 to peg 5. Knit 2 over 1 when working row and move loops in to fill gap).

Row 65: S1, P11, K1 (Dec is still worked on peg 4, but you will P2tog)

Row 66: S1, K11 (Dec is still worked on peg 4, but you will K2tog)

Row 67: S1, P9, K1 (Dec is still worked on peg 4, but you will P2tog)

BBO all pegs. Weave in all ends and trim close to work.

Closure strap

Using the fourth color of yarn (that you haven't yet used for your other panels), CCO 3 pegs. Leave a 10" tail for seaming. Work as a flat panel.

Repeat in the following 2-row pattern until you've reached 8" in length. The closure strap is shorter than the panel is wide so that there will be a little negative ease to help keep the closure flap in place:

> **Row a:** S1, K2
>
> **Row b:** S1, P1, K1

BBO all 3 pegs. Leave a 10" tail for seaming.

Assembly

Lay the Closure Strap on top of the Front Panel, just underneath the garter stitching. Using the CO and BO tails from your closure strap, stitch it in place at the

ends only. Keep just a little bit of the strap overhanging the Front Panel on each end while stitching.

Pin the Front Panel to the circular Strap Panel so that one of the strap's seams is centered at the bottom of the Front Panel. Make sure to tuck the overhanging ends of the Closure Strap to what will be the inside of the bag. Stitch pieces together using one of the four colors of yarn: sample uses a decorative blanket stitch, but a whipstitch could also be used.

Pin the Back Panel in place so that everything lines up evenly. Stitch in place using the same method as before. Continue the decorative stitching all the way up both sides of the strap, using the same color yarn.

If desired, add a little decorative button to the side of the Closure Strap.

Block well, using a square form that fits inside the bag snuggly to help permanently set the shape.

Now put your set to good use and head out on a walkabout!

Lacy Heirloom Pillow

 EASY  MEDIUM

Whether this is used as a treasured bit of luxury in a girl's bedroom, or for a little guy during his very important job as ring bearer, the design of the delicate-yet-simple stitches will make this a cherished item for years to come.

Finished Size

Pillow = 9"x 9" (not including ruffle)

Needed

- Large-gauge loom with at least 24 pegs: blue round 24-peg Knifty Knitter loom used in sample.
- Worsted Weight yarn: less than 1 skein: Red Heart Shimmer in Snow used in sample, 97% acrylic, 3% metallic polyester, 280 yards per skein.
- 9" x 9" Decorative or Ring Bearer's Pillow (can be pre-made or one you make yourself.) If you can't find a pillow sized 9" x 9", you can go up to 10" in either direction, as the panel overlay will stretch a bit.
- Loom tool, crochet hook, tapestry needle, sewing needle and thread.
- Ribbon/Embellishments if desired.

If making your own pillow ...

- ½ Yard of Satin Fabric
- 1 ½ - 2 Yards of 2 ½" wide satin ribbon for ruffle
- 20" of 1 ¾" wide ribbon for hand strap (for use as a ring bearer pillow)
- Stuffing: a pillow form, or folded batting work the best, but regular stuffing can also be used.
- Sewing machine (not absolutely necessary, but very helpful!)

Notes

Techniques used: E-Wrap, Purl, Crochet CO, Basic BO, Basic Sewing Skills.

This pattern uses one strand of yarn held throughout.

Step by step

Crochet CO 24 pegs as a flat panel.

Knit in the following pattern:

Row 1: S1, EW23

Row 2: S1, P22, EW1

Row 3: Repeat Row 1

Row 4: Repeat Row 2

Row 5: S1, EW2, Pegs 4-21 repeat: (EW1, S1, EW1, P1, S1, P1), Pegs 22-24: EW3

Row 6: S1, P2, Pegs 21-4 repeat: (EW3, P1, EW1, P1), Pegs 3-1: P2, EW1

Rows 7-51: Repeat Rows 5 & 6

Rows 52-55: Repeat Rows 1-4

Basic BO.

Block lightly if desired, pinning to the final desired measurement to match your pillow top.

Pin panel to top of pillow, then tack in place with sewing needle and thread. Embellish as desired.

If you're making your own pillow, cut two, 10" squares from satin.

Gather your length of 2½" ribbon using 2 lengths of basting stitches along one long edge, then stitch gathered ribbon to right side of one square, keeping edges even.

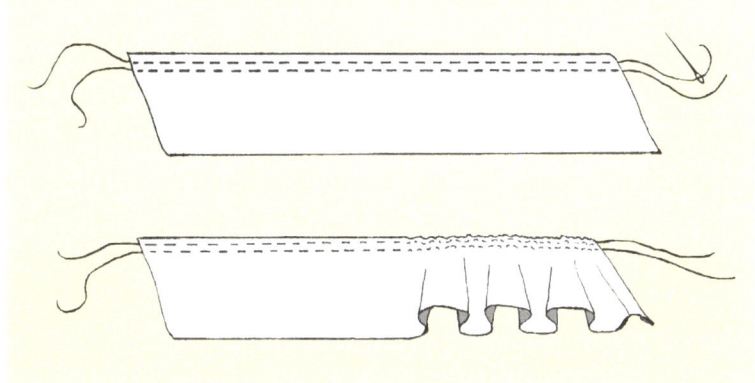

Lacy Heirloom Pillow, cont.

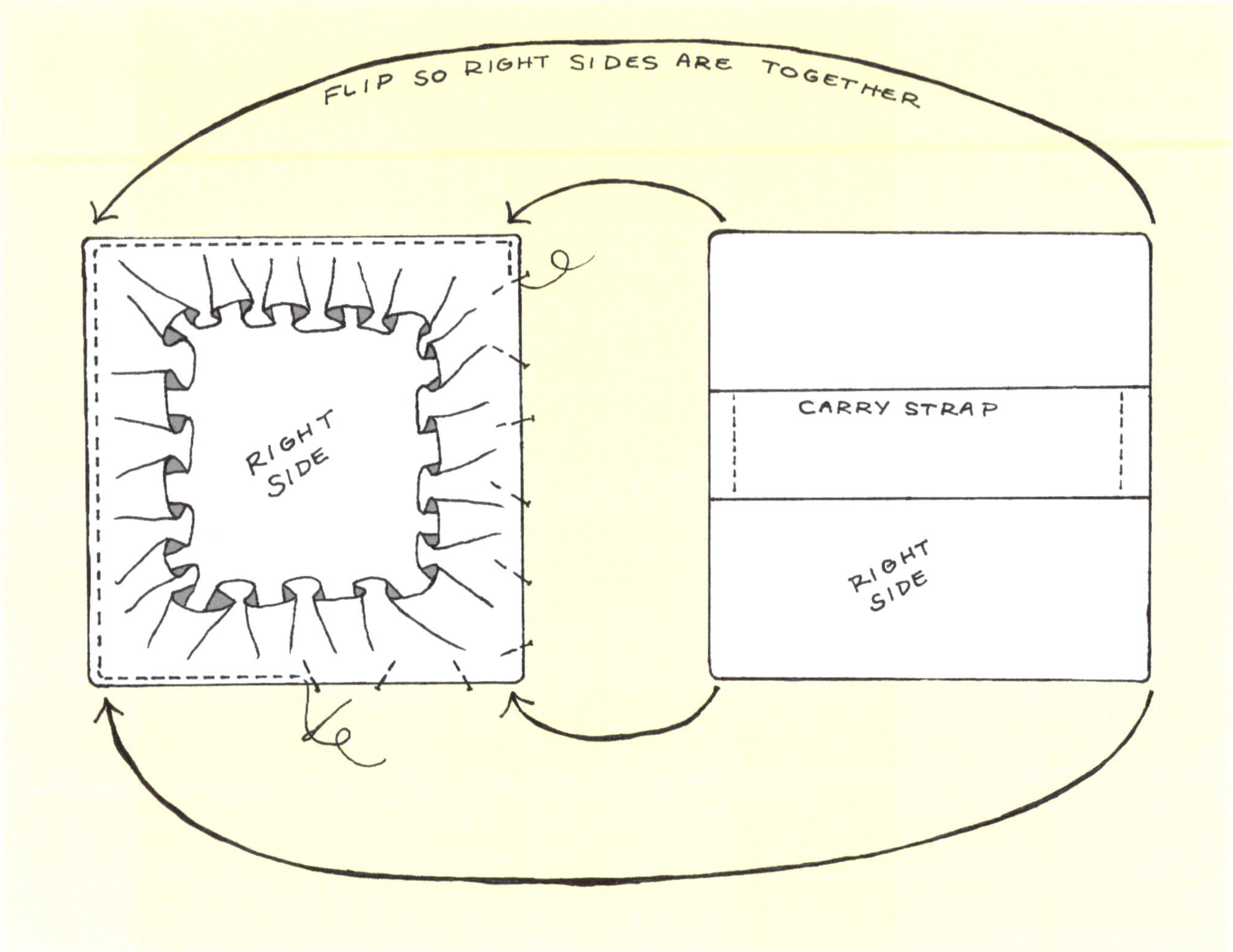

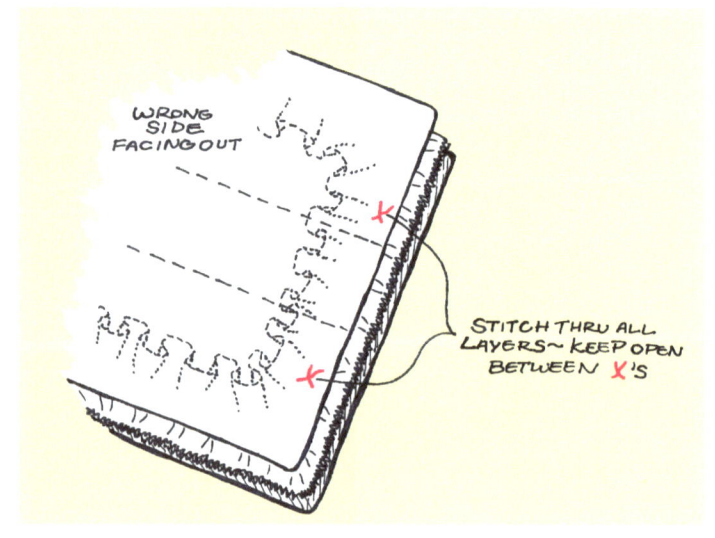

For use as a ring bearer's pillow, pin length of ribbon across the right side of other square for hand strap, then stitch securely in place on outside edges.

Pin right sides of squares together, keeping gathered ribbon sandwiched inside the 2 squares and free of edges, then carefully stitch around pillow at approx. 5/8" from edge, making sure to keep 2/3 of one side open for stuffing.

After turning pillow right side out and stuffing, neatly topstitch open side closed. Attach your loom knitted panel, adding any additional embellishments as desired.

ELSEWHERE IN THE BOOK ...
Doll Duds
Pages 88-93

Rosette Bunny Band

Bear Hat

Bunny's Frilly Skirt

Bear Pull-Over

Bunny Shoes and Bear Booties

A Pair of Lacy Trims

MODERATE SUPER FINE BULKY

These lovely lacy trims are the perfect embellishment for all those items that need that little extra touch; from hats and blankets to socks and mitts. Make them on any size loom to create the perfect width, tailor-made for each project.

Cabled Lacy Trim

Finished Size

Extra-fine gauge: 12 rows will yield approx. 1" in length x 1 1/8" wide

Large gauge: 2" per 10 rows x 3.5" wide 10 rows will yield approx. 2" in length by 3.5" wide

Needed

- Any size loom with at least 10 pegs: extra fine gauge Sock Loom by Décor Accents Inc. and blue round 24-peg Knifty Knitter were used in samples.
- #1 Sock Weight yarn: approx. 1/3 skein Patons Kroy Socks, Jacquards in Country Jacquard used in hat sample; 75% washable wool, 25% nylon, 166 yards per skein.
- #5 Chunky Weight yarn: approx. 2/3 skein Bernat Softee Chunky, in Nature's Way used in blanket sample; 100% acrylic, 134 yards per skein.
- Loom tool, crochet hook, cable needle, tapestry needle, sewing needle and thread.

Notes

Techniques used: Knit, Purl, Crochet CO, Purl 2 Together, Yarn Over, 2 Stitch Left Cross Cable, basic sewing skills.

This pattern uses one strand of yarn held throughout. All Knit Stitches are worked as U-Stitches.

Four-row repeated pattern

Row 1: S1, K1, YO, P2tog, K2, P1, YO, P2tog, P1

Row 2: (on peg 1 of row: K2) K1, YO, P2tog, 2StLC, P1, YO, P2tog, P1

Row 3: (on peg 1 of row: K2) K1, YO, P2tog, K2, P1, YO P2tog, P1

Row 4: S1, K1, YO P2tog, 2StLC, P1, YO, P2tog, P1

Let's break it down

Crochet CO 10 pegs from right to left.

Row 1: Slip the first peg, knit the second. Move the loop from peg 3 to peg 4. Carry the yarn across the front of peg 3 and purl the two loops as one on peg 4. Knit pegs 5 & 6. Purl peg 7. Move the loop from peg 8 to peg 9. Carry the yarn across the front of peg 8 and purl the two loops as one on peg 9. Purl peg 10.

Row 2: On peg 1, knit one stitch, then come back around peg 1 to knit another stitch. Knit peg 2. Move the loop from peg 3 to peg 4. Carry the yarn across the front of peg 3 and purl the two loops as one of peg 4. Place the loop from peg 6 on a cable needle. Move the loop from peg 5 to peg 6. Replace the loop from the cable needle to peg 5. Knit pegs 5 and 6. Purl peg 7. Move the loop from peg 8 to peg 9. Carry the yarn across the front of peg 8 and purl the two loops as one on peg 9. Purl peg 10.

Cabled Lacy Trim, cont.

Row 3: On peg 1, knit one stitch, then come back around peg 1 to knit another stitch. Knit peg 2. Move the loop from peg 3 to peg 4. Carry the yarn across the front of peg 3 and purl the two loops as one on peg 4. Knit pegs 5 and 6. Purl peg 7. Move the loop from peg 8 to peg 9. Carry the yarn across the front of peg 8 and purl the two loops as one on peg 9. Purl peg 10.

Row 4: Slip the first peg, knit the second. Move the loop from peg 3 to peg 4. Carry the yarn across the front of peg 3 and purl the two loops as one on peg 4. Place the loop from peg 6 on a cable needle. Move the loop from peg 5 to peg 6. Replace the loop from the cable needle to peg 5. Knit pegs 5 and 6. Purl peg 7. Move the loop from peg 8 to peg 9. Carry the yarn across the front of peg 8 and purl the two loops as one on peg 9. Purl peg 10.

Repeat these four rows until your desired length has been achieved.

Basic BO all 10 stitches. Weave in tails. Block to hold shape and to pull lacy places open.

Stitch invisibly in place onto your project using needle and thread. Make sure to allow for some stretch in the knitted fabrics.

MAKIN' IT EASY!

Both of these lacy patterns use a specific number of rows to create the design, which are then repeated for the length needed for your trim. You can make sure that you have enough length for your item by using one of two ways. You can simply measure the edges of the project and knit your lace to that length, or you can knit a portion of the lace and stitch it in place onto your project as you knit, continuing in this manner until your embellishment is complete. This second way is very useful when working the borders around corners.

Lacy Scalloped Trim

Finished size

Extra-fine gauge: 16 rows will yield approx. 1.25" in length by 1.25" wide

Large gauge: 16 rows will yield approx. 3" in length by 4.5" wide

Needed

- Any size loom with at least 11 pegs for hat version and 17 pegs for blanket version: extra-fine-gauge sock loom by Décor Accents Inc. and blue round 24-peg Knifty Knitter were used in samples.
- #1 Sock Weight yarn: approx. 1/3 skein Patons Kroy Socks, Jacquards in Fern Rose Jacquard used in hat sample; 75% washable wool, 25% nylon, 166 yards per skein.
- #4 Worsted Weight yarn: approx. 2 skeins Vanna's Choice Baby, in Lamb used in blanket sample; 100% acrylic, 170 yards per skein.
- Loom tool, crochet hook, tapestry needle, sewing needle and thread.

Notes

Techniques used: Knit, Purl, Crochet CO, Knit 2 Together, Purl 2 Together, Yarn Over, basic sewing skills, I-Cord Seaming.

This pattern uses one strand of yarn held throughout. All Knit Stitches are worked as U-Stitches.

Eight-row repeated pattern (as shown on gold hat):

[16-row repeated pattern] (as shown on Cozy Crib Blanket):

Set-up row: K3, YO, K2tog, [P2, K2, P2] YO2, K2tog, K1 (9 [15] pegs)

*¨ Row 1: P3, K1, [P2, K2, P2] P2, YO, P2tog, P1

Row 2: S1, K2, YO, K2tog, [P2, K2, P2] K1, YO2, K2tog, K1 (10 [16] pegs)

Row 3: P3, K1, P1, [P2, K2, P2] P2, YO, P2tog, P1

Row 4: S1, K2, YO, K2tog, [P2, K2, P2] K2, YO2, K2tog, K1 (11 [17] pegs)

Row 5: P3, K1, P2, [P2, K2, P2] P2, YO, P2tog, P1

Row 6: S1, K2, YO, K2tog, [P2, K2, P2] K6

Row 7: BBO 3 sts, P2, [P2, K2, P2] P2, YO, P2tog, P1 (8 [14] pegs)

Row 8: S1, K2, YO, K2tog, [P2, K2, P2] YO2, K2tog, K1 (9 [15] pegs) *

The following 8 rows are only for the 16-row pattern:

[Row 9: P3, K1, [P1, K1, P2, K1, P1] P2, YO, P2tog, P1

Row 10: S1, K2, YO, K2tog, [P1, K1, P2, K1, P1] K1, YO2, K2tog, K1 [16 pegs]

Row 11: P3, K1, P1, [P1, K1, P2, K1, P1] P2, YO, P2tog, P1

Row 12: S1, K2, YO, K2tog, [P1, K1, P2, K1, P1] K2, YO2, K2tog, K1 [17 pegs]

Row 13: P3, K1, P2, [P1, K1, P2, K1, P1] P2, YO, P2tog, P1

Row 14: S1, K2, YO, K2tog, [P1, K1, P2, K1, P1] K6

Row 15: BBO 3 sts, P2, [P1, K1, P2, K1, P1] P2, YO, P2tog, P1 [14 pegs]

Row 16: S1, K2, YO, K2tog, YO2, K2tog, K1 [15 pegs]] ¨

8-row pattern: Repeat steps inside * until desired length

16-row pattern: Repeat steps inside ¨ until desired length

Let's break it down

Crochet CO 8 [14] pegs from left to right.

Set-up row: (right to left) Knit the first 3 pegs. Move the loop from the 4th peg to peg 5. Carry the yarn across the front of peg 4 and knit the two loops as one on peg 5. [repeated ribbing sts: P2, K2, P2] Move the last loop over to increase by one peg. Move the 2nd to last loop over, next to the last loop. Move the 3rd to last loop on top of the 2nd to last loop. You will now have 2 empty pegs. Carry the yarn across the front of both of these pegs. Knit 2 loops as one on the next peg. Knit the last peg. You should now have 9 [15] pegs in use.

65

Lacy Scalloped Trim, cont.

Row 1: (left to right) Purl the first 3 pegs. Knit peg 4. [repeated ribbing sts: P2, K2, P2] Purl 2 pegs. Move the loop from the next peg over one peg to the right. Carry the yarn across the front of the now empty peg and purl the two loops as one. Purl the last peg.

Row 2: (right to left) Slip the first peg, knit the next 2 pegs. Move the loop from the 4th peg to peg 5. Carry the yarn across the front of peg 4 and knit the two loops as one on peg 5. [repeated ribbing sts: P2, K2, P2] Knit one. Move the last loop over to increase by one peg. Move the 2nd to last loop over, next to the last loop. Move the 3rd to last loop on top of the 2nd to last loop. You will now have 2 empty pegs. Carry the yarn across the front of both of these pegs. Knit 2 loops as one on the next peg. Knit the last peg. You should now have 10 [16] pegs in use.

Row 3: (left to right) Purl the first 3 pegs. Knit peg 4. Purl peg 5. [repeated ribbing sts: P2, K2, P2] Purl 2 pegs. Move the loop from the next peg over one peg to the right. Carry the yarn across the front of the now empty peg and purl the two loops as one. Purl the last peg.

Row 4: (right to left) Slip the first peg, knit the next 2 pegs. Move the loop from the 4th peg to peg 5. Carry the yarn across the front of peg 4 and knit the two loops as one on peg 5. [repeated ribbing sts: P2, K2, P2] Knit 2. Move the last loop over to increase by one peg. Move the 2nd to last loop over, next to the last loop. Move the 3rd to last loop on top of the 2nd to last loop. You will now have 2 empty pegs. Carry the yarn across the front of both of these pegs. Knit 2 loops as one on the next peg. Knit the last peg. You should now have 11 [17] pegs in use.

Row 5: (left to right) Purl the first 3 pegs. Knit peg 4. Purl pegs 5 and 6, [repeated ribbing sts: P2, K2, P2] Purl 2 pegs. Move the loop from the next peg over one peg to the right. Carry the yarn across the front of the now empty peg and purl the two loops as one. Purl the last peg.

Row 6: (right to left) Slip the first peg, knit the next 2 pegs. Move the loop from the 4th peg to peg 5. Carry the yarn across the front of peg 4 and knit the two loops as one on peg 5. [repeated ribbing sts: P2, K2, P2] Knit all remaining six pegs.

Row 7: (left to right) Basic BO the first 3 pegs until you are left with your original number of CO pegs. Purl the next 2 pegs, [repeated ribbing sts: P2, K2, P2] Purl 2 pegs. Move the loop from the next peg over one peg to the right. Carry the yarn across the front of the now empty peg and purl the two loops as one. Purl the last peg. You should now have 8 [14] pegs with loops.

Row 8: (right to left) Slip the first peg, knit the next 2 pegs. Move the loop from the 4th peg to peg 5. Carry the yarn across the front of peg 4 and knit the two loops as one on peg 5. [repeated ribbing sts: P2, K2, P2] Move the last loop over to increase by one peg. Move the 2nd to last loop over, next to the last loop. Move the 3rd to last loop on top of the 2nd to last loop. You will now have 2 empty pegs. Carry the yarn across the front of both of these pegs. Knit 2 loops as one on the next peg. Knit the last peg. You should now have 9 [15] pegs in use.

[Rows 9-16: repeat the same 8 rows as above, leaving out the set up row, and inserting the next set of repeated ribbing sts: [P1, K1, P2, K1, P1] in place of the ones detailed in rows 1-8.]

Repeat these 8 [16] rows until your desired length has been achieved.

Basic BO all pegs. Weave in tails. Block to hold shape and to pull lacy places open.

When using as an appliqué trim, stitch invisibly in place onto your project using needle and thread. Make sure to allow for some stretch in the knitted fabrics. To use as a trim on a knitted piece, mattress stitch in place, or use the I-Cord Seaming technique (Page 69) for an added decorative raised border (as shown on Cozy Crib Blanket).

Cozy Crib Blanket

When combining the wonderfully soft and stretchy honeycomb stitch with the lovely Lacy Scalloped Trim, the resulting blanket is sure to become someone's favorite cuddle-time treasure!

Finished Size

(All measures are approximate, as the blanket does stretch.)

33"x 41" with Lacy Scalloped Trim, found on Page 65.

Blanket gauge: 3 $\frac{1}{3}$ sts x 5 rows per inch

Trim gauge: 16 rows will yield 3" in length by 4.5" wide

Needed

LOOMS

- **Blanket:** Any loom which can be used for double knitting in the gauge you prefer: Décor Accents, Inc. small-gauge afghan board was used in sample.
- **Trim:** Any Large-gauge loom with at least 17 pegs; blue round 24-peg Knifty Knitter was used in sample.

YARN

- **Blanket:** Worsted Weight yarn: 3 skeins Plymouth Yarn's Encore Colorspun in Prints, Color #7115 used in sample; 75% acrylic, 25% wool, 200 yards per skein.
- **Trim:** #4 Worsted Weight yarn: approx. 2 skeins Vanna's Choice Baby, in Lamb used in blanket sample; 100% acrylic, 170 yards per skein.
- Loom tool, crochet hook, tapestry needle

Notes

Techniques used: Honeycomb Stitch, Knit, Purl, Crochet CO, Knit 2 Together, Purl 2 Together, Yarn Over, I-Cord Seaming.

This pattern uses one strand of yarn held throughout. In making the trim, all Knit Stitches are worked as U-Stitches.

Step by step

CO using one strand of yarn in the following honeycomb stitch pattern, onto the number of pegs you've decided to use (sample used 30 peg pairs/60 pegs total):

CO: EW 2 pegs in line, * then move across to the other side of the loom and EW the next 2 pegs in line. Repeat from * to the end of the row:

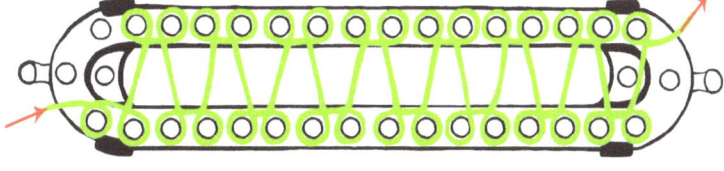

Turn: At the end of the row, turn for the start of the next row by bringing your WY straight to the peg directly across from the last one wrapped, to the inside of the last peg pairs. Wrap around that peg, then continue to wrap around the next peg in line using the same method as before:

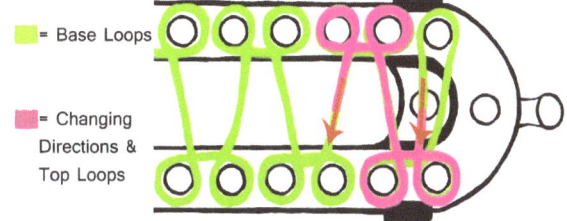

Cozy Crib Blanket, cont.

Row 1: Continue across the row in the same pattern as used for the CO, so that you will now have 2 loops on the pegs that have previously been wrapped. KO.

Rows 2-5: Repeat Row 1.

Rows 6-10: EW pegs in the opposite pattern as before, alternating the peg pairs that you've been knitting so that the connecting lines between the pegs are now stretching across the places where there were none on the previous rows. KO.

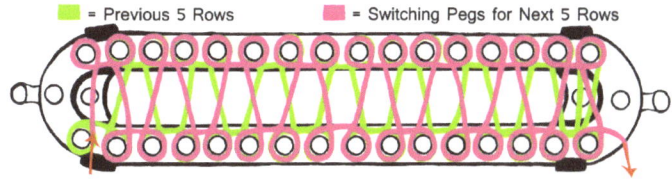

Note: *A helpful way to keep track of row counts is to count a row every time you KO, rather than each time you wrap.*

Continue in this manner, alternating the pegs being wrapped every 5 rows, until you've reached your desired length: sample used 31 repeats for a total of 155 rows.

Double Knit BO all pegs & employ the CO finishing techniques found on Page 108.

Complete the needed length of the Lacy Scalloped Trim, following the pattern on Page 65.

I-Cord seaming

This technique is a great way to piece two knitted sections together, while creating a raised I-Cord running along the top of the seam all in one step!

You will accomplish this by seaming at the top side of the blanket, making it nearly invisible from the bottom side.

Note: *The finished result of this technique is fairly NONELASTIC! You would therefore need to keep your stitches loose as they are worked, so that your blanket edges are not pulled too tightly. You'll want a bit of stretch to the finished border.*

Line up the pieces to be seamed side by side, pinning in place if necessary. I've found this process works best if you work on top of a carpet, or something that naturally keeps the pieces from moving out of position.

MAKIN' IT EASY!

The beauty of this pattern is that you can work with pretty much any gauge loom. You could easily work this up on a Knifty Knitter long loom, and if the piece is not wide enough, simply make additional panels and stitch them together! I would recommend making a swatch of your blanket before hand to see how many pegs/panels you will need to achieve your desired finished measurement.

You will be using a loom of the same (or larger) gauge as that which you've knitted your project with. The sample uses a section piece of a Décor Accents loom for ease of use during this technique, but any loom will work.

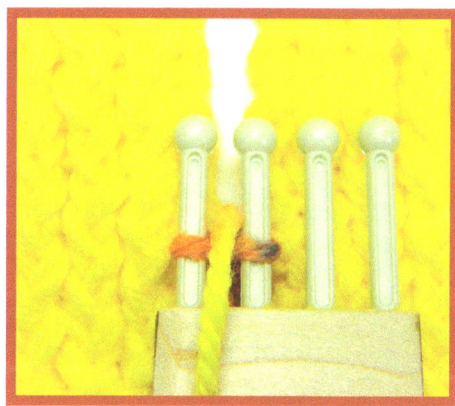

Begin by placing a loose slip knot from your WY onto the first peg. EW peg 2 twice. Wrap back around peg 1. KO both pegs. You have now set up your loom for the I-Cord Seaming.

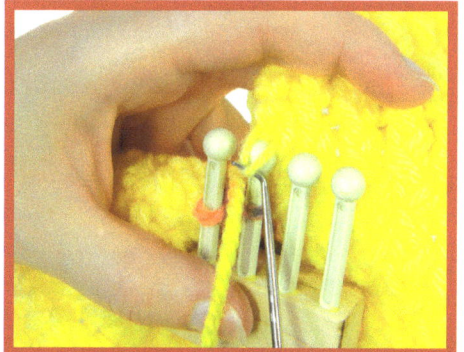

*From inside the edging of the right-hand piece to be seamed, pull the first knitted loop up onto the right peg, above the set-up loop.

Cozy Crib Blanket, cont.

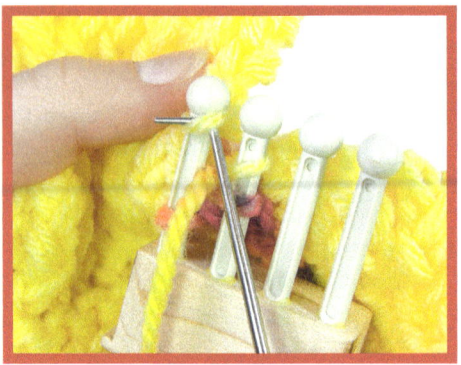

Pull the first loop from the inside edging of the left-hand piece to be seamed up onto the left peg, above the set-up loop.

Note: When seaming the corners, tuck and pin the trim into three folded pleats to allow the lace to lay flat. When I-Cord Seaming this area, make sure to pull up an inside loop from each layer of the individual folds for each stitch. This can be up to a total of 3 loops pulled onto the trim side of the I-Cord, plus the base loop. The blanket side will still have just the one loop, plus the base loop. KO all the extra layers over the very top loop of the peg, leaving just one base loop each time.

Bind Off using Basic BO. Seam your 2 trim edges together invisibly. Block blanket with the Lacy Scalloped Trim pinned open to show the beautiful lace at its best.

Wrap the WY around both pegs in a figure-eight motion, as if you are knitting an I-Cord.

Knit off 2 loops over 1 on each of the pegs.

Give a little tug to the freshly KO stitches to help loosen the tension.

Repeat from *, until your seaming is complete.

play things

Felted Art Satchel

EASY MEDIUM BULKY

This is the perfect travel companion for your little budding artist! The durable felted fabric will last through all kinds of wear and tear and the big pockets make carrying those important crafty items a cinch. Everyone around will want to join in and let the creative juices flow.

Finished Size

14" in height; 10.75" width; 28" total length when opened flat.

Gauge

2.5 sts (S) x 3.5 rows (R) per inch (before felting)

See Gauge and Size Calculators, Page 5

Needed

- Large-gauge loom with at least 36 pegs: 36 peg green round Knifty Knitter used in sample.
- #4 Worsted Weight yarn in 2 coordinating colors — Patons Classic Wool used in sample; 100% wool, 223 yards per skein; approx. 3 skeins in burgundy and approx. 1½ skeins in pumpkin.
- #5 Bulky Weight yarn in 6 coordinating colors – Knit Picks Wool of the Andes used in sample; 100% wool, 137 yards per skein; approx. ½ skein of each color in sky, turmeric, chocolate, masala, natural and oregano.
- For the inside panel, button strap and the handles: Sample uses 2 strands of the #4 worsted weight yarn, in coordinating colors, held together as one.
- For the outside of the satchel and for the inside pockets: Sample uses one strand of the same color of the #4 worsted weight yarn held together with 1 strand of the #5 bulky weight yarn, switching of the bulky yarn directed in the pattern.
- Large button for closure (sample uses a 1³⁄₈" button).
- Loom tool, 6.5 mm crochet hook, tapestry needle, knitting marking pins, sharp scissors, hot water/washing machine, laundry bag, and 1 tbsp laundry soap for felting.
- **Optional:** If you'd like to embellish the front of the satchel, you can use such items as decorative buttons, patches, crafting felt and embroidery thread. Hot glue is great for adhering these items.
- You might also want to have an 8.5" x 11" top-bound drawing pad and some art supplies for filling the pockets.

Notes

Techniques used: E-Wrap, Panel Knit, Crochet CO, Basic BO, Decreasing, Seaming, Felting.

This pattern uses two strands of yarn held throughout, as described in the yarn requirements section.

Step by step

Front panel

Using 1 strand of worsted weight yarn held together with 1 strand of bulky weight yarn, CCO 36 pegs. Work as a flat panel.

Rows 1-115: EW all pegs. Create random stripes with your bulky weight yarns as you knit, holding each stripe's color together with the same color of worsted weight yarn throughout for continuity.

BBO all pegs. This should result in a panel of approx. 34" x 15"

Pockets

Create two more panels using the exact same method as used in the Front Panel, with each panel using all 36 pegs, but knit only 25 rows for each pocket panel.

Inside panel

Using 1 strand each of the 2 colors of worsted weight yarns, CCO 36 pegs. Work as a flat panel.

Rows 1-115: EW all pegs.

BBO all pegs.

Felted Art Satchel, cont.

Button strap

Using 1 strand each of the 2 colors of worsted weight yarns, CCO 12 pegs. Work as a flat panel.

Rows 1-25: S1, EW11.

Rows 26-44: S1, EW1, D1, EW remaining pegs. Dec. 1 st each row until all pegs are BO.

Handles

*Using 1 strand each of the 2 colors of worsted weight yarns, CCO 8 pegs. Work as a flat panel.

Rows 1-60: S1, EW7.

BBO all pegs.

Repeat from * to create one more handle.

Finishing

Seam both front and inside panels together around all edges.

Pin the 2 pocket panels in place on what will be the inside-front half of the satchel when folded. Seam the pockets in place. Make a seam up the center of the top pocket to create 2 smaller pockets.

Pin the 2 handles on the outside top edges of the folded satchel. Stitch evenly and securely in place all the way to the top edge of the satchel.

Pin the button strap at the center-top of the back panel, just a little lower than the straps. Stitch securely in place all the way to the top edge of the satchel.

Felt the satchel as detailed on Page 111.

Keep checking during the felting process to make sure that you do not over-felt the piece, resulting in your art supplies not fitting inside!

Once your satchel is felted to the correct size, stretch and shape all the sections to the desired form and let it dry. Make sure to keep checking the progress of the satchel as it dries to keep shaping and molding during the setting process.

On the inside of the back half of the satchel, cut a slit about 1" down from the top, and 1" in on each side for the cardboard backing of your drawing pad to slide into. Before you cut, make sure of the placement needed for this cut by comparing it to your drawing pad. The felting process may have made your measurements slightly different than the sample.

Felted Art Satchel, cont.

Using the color of yarn you desire for accent, blanket stitch entirely around this opening.

Fill your satchel with your art supplies. Close the satchel and pull up the button strap, as if it was being buttoned. Measure to determine where you'd like the button and buttonhole to be. Stitch the button in place on the front-outside half of the satchel. Cut a buttonhole in the corresponding place on the button strap. Blanket stitch around the buttonhole opening, using the same color as you've used for the drawing pad opening.

Embellish the front as desired. Letter templates are provided below, if you'd like to photocopy them to use as a pattern in making your own letters out of crafter's felt. In the sample, each letter was embroidered with a running stitch and then hot-glued in place. Buttons and a decorative appliqué patch were also added to the sample.

Koby the Striped Kitty

MODERATE MEDIUM

This little guy just melts my heart. He's such a sweet thing with all his striped and floppy goodness. He's sure to make long lasting friendships wherever he goes!

Finished Size

Standing Height: 22"

Sitting Height: 12"

Sitting Width: 7"

Sitting Depth with Tail: 20"

Needed

- Large-gauge adjustable loom with at least 26 pegs: pink long Knifty Knitter with loom clips used in sample.
- Worsted Weight yarn in 4 colors: 1 skein each, with one extra for body/head color: Vanna's Choice by Lion Brand used in sample in taupe mist, denim mist, scarlet, and fern, 100% acrylic, 170 yards per skein. A very small portion of black yarn was used in embroidering the face.
- Stuffing: both cluster type polyfill and scrap yarn were used in sample. Queen-size pantyhose in nude were used in containing polyfill.
- Loom tool, crochet hook, tapestry needle
- Buttons or child-safe eyes, and ribbon if desired.

Notes

Techniques used: Flat Knit/U-Stitch, Drawstring CO, Gathered BO, Basic BO, Short Rows, Increase/Decrease, Embroidery.

This pattern uses one strand of yarn held throughout.

All CO and BO tails should be about 20" in length for use in stitching pieces together. After seaming, the trimmed ends can be added to polyfill when stuffing your kitty.

Step by step

Body

Using body color, Drawstring CO 26 pegs to work in the round.

FK 40 rows.

Decrease one stitch every row, alternating opposing sides of each round, until 12 pegs are left with loops, adjusting loops and loom clips as necessary.

Gather BO, leave open.

Cinch CO end closed tightly and knot.

Stuff: Place a closed end (the toe or knotted end) of pantyhose inside body, folding other end over top of body. Fill firmly with cluster polyfill. Knot and trim pantyhose when filled completely. Cinch top of body closed and knot.

Koby the Striped Cat, cont.

Head

Using head/body color, Drawstring CO 26 pegs to work in the round.

FK 40 rows.

Gather BO, leave open.

Cinch CO end closed tightly and knot.

(If you desire to use child-safe eyes, this is the point you'll need to apply them: before stuffing and knotting head closed.)

Stuff in the same manner as the body, knot and trim the pantyhose, but leave this end uncinched until assembly.

Legs (Make 4)

Read through Makin' It Easy! boxes #1, #2 and #3 for ideas to help make creating those stripes a simple and successful process.

Using the loom clips, set the loom at 12 pegs. With your first stripe color, Drawstring CO all 12 pegs to work in the round.

FK in the round, changing colors every two rows, following a 4-color pattern repeat. Complete 5 repeats of the 4-color pattern, ending with 2 rows of your starting color, for a total of 42 rows.

Gather BO, but leave open until assembly. Stuff either using Makin' It Easy! #3, or with polyfill stuffed pantyhose. The legs should be slightly floppy.

Tail

Use the same procedure as the legs.

At the start of the 6th 4-color repeat (Row 41) you'll begin making short rows to create the crook in the tail:

Note: *Make sure to keep making color changes during short rows!*

FK pegs 1-6. Lift loop from peg 7 and wrap & turn.

FK pegs 6-1. Lift loop from peg 12 and wrap & turn using next stripe color.

FK pegs 1-5. Lift loop from peg 6 and wrap & turn.

FK pegs 5-2. Lift loop from peg 1 and wrap & turn using next stripe color.

Continue decreasing in this way until only 2 pegs are left unwrapped. Begin short row increases until all wrapped

MAKIN' IT EASY! #1

In making the 4-colored stripes, you can pull the colors up and use them again without cutting yarn! This saves a lot of effort in weaving in ends later. The colors not being used are just carried up through the inside of the tube and won't show through at all. Just give a little tug to the stitches you've previously created with the carry up yarn before bringing that yarn up and over all the other color strands, making sure not to pull so tightly that your piece becomes puckered. If you end up with a loose space along the place where the yarn is carried up, you can use a little running stitch during seaming to tighten this area up a bit.

pegs have been knit off and you're back to the first stripe color from Row 41. (Page 106)

FK one more 4-color pattern repeat (8 rows).

FK 4 rows of tail tip color.

Begin to decrease one stitch every row, alternating opposing sides of each round to keep the point of the tail even. Repeat until all pegs are BO, moving loops and clips as necessary.

Stuff either using Makin' It Easy! #3, or with polyfill stuffed pantyhose.

Koby the Striped Cat, cont.

MAKIN' IT EASY! #2

Place your balls of yarn in your tote or basket in order of the color pattern you will be using. When you're working on one color, this ball can be taken from the rest and set next to you. When you're ready for the next color, place this ball last in the line and grab the next color of the pattern, which should be the first in line. In doing this, you will be able to keep all those connected strands from getting tangled and save yourself from a major headache!

Ears (Make 2)

Using the loom clips, set the loom at 14 pegs. With your first stripe color, Drawstring CO all 14 pegs to work in the round.

Rows 1-14: FK 14 rows in your 4-color stripe pattern.

Rows 15-18: Decreases are worked every row, alternating them at opposite sides of the round until 10 pegs remain.

Gather BO. Finish & stuff as in Makin' It Easy! #3.

Using CO tail, create a vertical running stitch in the center of ear front and pull to give the ear some curve.

Feet (Make 4)

Using loom clips, set loom for 20 pegs with the clips at each end, so that the clip pegs are even with the loom pegs and form a square, rather than an oval. With one of the stripe colors, AdjCO 9 pegs of one side of the loom, not including loom clips.

PFK 12 rows.

Pull the CO edge over to the opposite side of the loom and place these stitches on the 9 pegs across from your knitting. It will help to start at the center sts, working your way out on each side from there. Pick up a stitch on each side of the panel and place the stitch on the single peg on each loom clip. All 20 pegs should now have stitches on them.

Note: Make sure to pull up outside loops of CO, not inside loops. Also, you may find success at eliminating extra gaps on the sides by pulling up 2 sts onto the end clips, rather than just 1. These 2 loops would then be knit together as one in the next row.

Working with all 20 pegs, FK 14 rounds.

Gather BO.

Pull in any slack across CO seam by pulling gently on CO tail. You can also whip stitch closed any extra spaces on the CO panel edges at this time. Knot and pull end to inside.

Koby the Striped Cat, cont.

Stuff as in Makin' It Easy! #3 or polyfill stuffed pantyhose, cinch tightly closed with BO tail, and knot.

Using BO tail, stitch 2 tight loops across toe area to create toe shapes, knotting as you go.

Belly

With one of the stripe colors, Crochet CO 4 pegs, positioned in the center of 10 pegs.

PFK Row 1.

PFK Row 2: move loop with WY over one peg so that there is an empty peg between first 2 loops. S1 (moved loop), M1 (pull up loop from previous row onto empty peg), K to the end of the row.

PFK Rows 3-7: Repeat Row 2, adding the number of knits after M1 to reflect growing number of pegs. You should end up with 10 pegs with loops.

PFK Rows 8-21: S1, K9

PFK Rows 22-27: decrease one stitch each row (move 2nd loop next to WY above 3rd loop, move WY loop over one peg to fill gap, knit 2 over 1 on 2nd peg in row):

S1, D1, knit remaining pegs. Repeat until you are left with 4 pegs with loops. BBO.

Muzzle

With one of the stripe colors, Drawstring CO 20 pegs to work in the round.

FK 10 rows.

Gather BO. Cinch tightly closed and knot.

Using BO tail, stitch a tight loop from the center gather to create mouth and cheek shapes, then knot.

Stuff using Makin' It Easy! #3, leaving tails free and gently pull CO tail until it forms a cupped mouth shape. (Yarn tail can now be stuffed inside.)

Finishing

MAKIN' IT EASY! #3

When making the striped pieces, make sure to leave longer tails, both for stitching and for stuffing! Leave out your first and last color tail for stitching, but the rest can be stuffed inside the piece, which helps fill in any gaps where regular stuffing might show through. If you are concerned with having enough yarn, you can also use some scrap yarn from another skein that coordinates with your project.

Most of the stitching, if not all, is done by using the long CO and BO tails left during the knitting process. After stitching each piece in place, feel free to pull ends of tails invisibly through to the inside of the stuffed pieces and trim close at the other side. After a bit of fluffing the end will disappear into the stuffing.

Place the topmost point of the body inside the open end of the head. Push the head down onto the body so that it will have strength and not flop when sitting

Koby the Striped Cat, cont.

upright. Pull on the head's drawstring tail to cinch lightly closed around body.

Using the body's yarn tail, stitch head snuggly in place. Pull the head's drawstring tail to cinch in just a bit more for neck shaping, then knot securely. Pull ends to inside.

Pin ears in place on upper sides of head. Pull ear CO tail just a bit to shape to head and then stitch in place. You can bring the ears to life with strategically placed stitches and a bit of tugging as needed after attaching them to the head.

Pin muzzle in place, stretching into shape as you go. Stitch securely with yarn tail. Whipstitch lip-split again to emphasize and then shape nose:

Pinch point of nose in your fingers while you stitch into 3 points around the pinched section in the shape of an upsidedown triangle 2 or 3 times. Pull snuggly on both the stitches and the pinched part until a triangular shaped nose forms.

Stretch and pin belly patch into place on body. Stitch securely with yarn tails.

Pin feet to lower ends of legs and stitch using legs' yarn tails. You can use the yarn tail to cinch and shape the ends of the legs while you pin in place. The position of hands should be at the tip end, opposite the toes. The position of feet should be at the same end, but more on top of the foot.

Pin arms, legs and tail into place on body, using yarn tails to cinch for shaping as desired. Arms will be situated up close to the join of the head and body. Legs and tail will be placed so that the kitty can sit upright. Stitch all pieces securely in place.

You can add buttons for eyes and belly button, or use black yarn for embroidering features, including filling in the nose shape with long stitches. One dot of cream colored yarn was stitched into each eye for a highlight that makes the face really come alive!

Make sure to add the highlight dots to the same side of the each eye (left or right) so he won't end up looking cross-eyed.

Whiskers are created by pulling lengths of black yarn through the cheeks, inserting and exiting at points where you wish them to "grow". Snag the thick stitches in the nose as you pull through to the other side to help hold firmly in place. Double knot the ends at the length you desire and trim.

You can now add a stylish ribbon around his neck, or whip up a snuggly scarf to keep him warm.

Silly Sidewinder

MODERATE   MEDIUM

This spunky guy was originally created for my little grand-nephew. I thought this silly snake would be just the perfect thing for an imaginative boy to while away playtime with. This snake is definitely a flashy one, sporting bright diamonds across its length; the result of the short-row wedges that make up the construction.

Finished size
Total length is approx.: 48" from tongue to tail x 8.5" in circumference.

Gauge
3 sts x 5.75 rows per inch

Needed
- Large-gauge adjustable loom with at least 21 pegs: Sample uses pink long 26-peg Knifty Knitter and loom clips.
- #4 Worsted Weight yarn in 3 coordinating colors — approx. 1 skein of each: Loops & Threads Impeccable in amethyst (MC), dark forest (CC1) and butterscotch (CC2) used in sample; 100% acrylic, 277 yards per skein. A very small amount of Loops & Threads Impeccable in rouge was used in sample for making the snake's eyes and tongue.
- Polyester batting (or fiberfill) and a pair of children's 4T tights.
- Loom tool, 6 mm crochet hook, tapestry needle, peg marker, sewing thread and needle.
- Optional: buttons, crafter's felt or puffy fabric paint for applying facial features.

Notes
Techniques used: U-Stitch, Purl, Crochet CO, Make One Increase, Knit 2 Together, Short Row Shaping, Seaming, Embroidery, Crochet.

This pattern uses two strands of yarn held throughout.

All Knits are worked as U-Stitches throughout pattern, unless noted otherwise.

Step by step

Head

Set the loom clips so that they are in an 18-peg configuration, centered on your loom. Using 2 strands of the color that will be the head (MC), CCO 10 pegs, starting at one loom clip and working your way to the other. Work as a flat panel.

Set-up Row 1: S1, K8, W&T at peg 10.

Set-up Row 2: Beginning at peg 9, K8, W&T at peg 1.

Repeat the 2 set-up rows, W&T'ing one peg closer to the center on each row (Page 106). Do this until only 2 pegs are left unwrapped. At this point, you should begin your increases until you have KO all the W&T's, except the wraps at both peg 1 and peg 10, which will be worked into the next row to close any holes that might have been left from the short rows.

Tuck the CO tail inside the little turned pocket just created. Pull the CO edge straight across to the other side of the loom. Place the CO loops over the directly adjacent pegs to fill all 8 empty pegs. You should now have 18 pegs filled and the cup shape should be stretched across the inside of the loom.

Rows 1-8: Work in the round. K all pegs. (Row 1: you will be knitting 2 over 1 on pegs 1 and 10.)

Row 9: M1 at each of the loom clips. K all pegs.

Row 10: K all pegs.

Row 11: M1 at each of the loom clips. K all pegs.

Rows 12-14: K all pegs.

Row 15: K pegs 1-13.

Lay aside your MC and change to the color you'd like for your snake's eye lids (CC1). Working with just pegs 14-21, create another Short Row panel, with the first W&T pegs being 21 and 14. Work as before, so that there are 2 pegs left unwrapped before making your increases.

When you are left with pegs 14 and 21 still wrapped, but all the others have been KO, complete the rest of Row 15 by again picking up your MC and knitting all pegs in line from peg 14 to 22. Trim your CC1 to 25".

Silly sidewinder, cont.

Rows 16 & 17: K all pegs, working in the round.

Row 18: K2tog at both clip pegs (move clips as needed). K remaining pegs.

Row 19: K all pegs.

Row 20: K2tog at both clip pegs. K remaining pegs. You should be back to 18 pegs with loops.

Row 21: K all pegs.

Short-row wedges

Let's make some wedges!

The diamond pattern for this snake is created by strategically placed groups of short rows, which make up individual wedges. The way these are stacked together create a zigzag shaped tube.

To make a short-row wedge (make sure to read through to Set Up before beginning to knit):

You will be working these as a flat panel, beginning with just 2 pegs, and increasing by one peg every two rows. This is how they're worked:

Rows 1 & 2: S1, K1.

Rows 3 & 4: S1, K2.

Rows 5 & 6: S1, K3.

Rows 7 & 8: S1, K4.

Rows 9 & 10: S1, K5.

Rows 11-36: continue in this same manner, knitting one additional peg per 2 rows.

After Row 36, you should be back at the 1st peg and with all 18 pegs having been worked with short rows. Trim WY.

There are 13 wedges that make up the snake's body. To get these wedges to line up correctly, you will be creating some of them starting at peg 1. The others will be started at peg 18 and will be worked in exactly in the mirror opposite direction. For those wedges, just consider peg 18 as your peg 1, peg 17 as your peg 2, etc.

The following instructions are for which direction to use for each wedge, as well as which colored yarn to use to achieve the diamond patterning:

Set Up: Using your MC, K pegs 1-5. Place your peg marker on peg 5. This is now your new peg 1. The peg

that was originally peg 6 will now be your new peg 18. This will place the first diamond point at the center of the underside of the snake body, right under his chin.

*Wedge One: Begin at peg 1.

    Rows 1-33: Work using MC.

    Rows 34-36: Work using CC1.

Wedge Two: Begin at peg 18.

    Rows 1-36: Work using CC2.

Wedge Three: Begin at peg 18.

    Rows 1-33: Work using CC2.

    Rows 34-36: Work using CC1.

Silly sidewinder, cont.

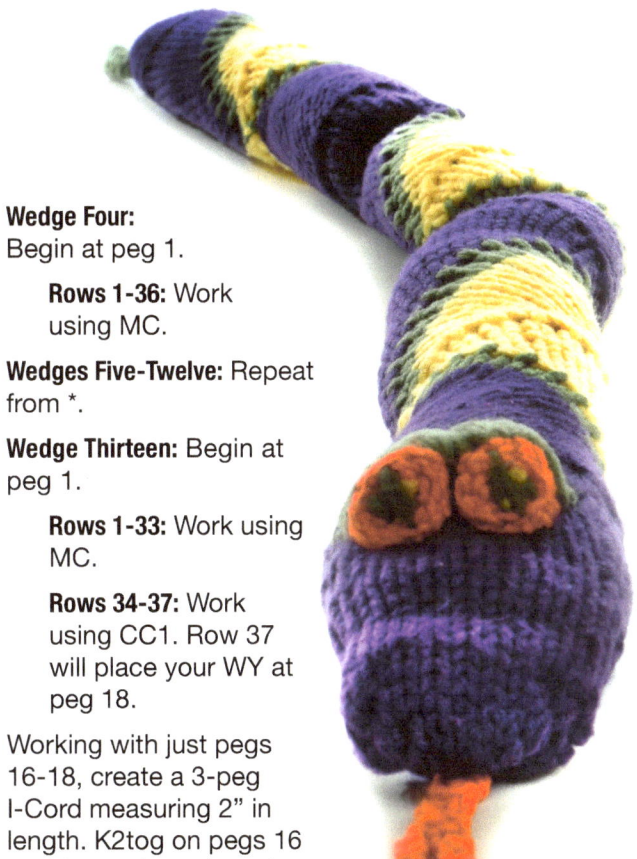

Wedge Four:
Begin at peg 1.

> **Rows 1-36:** Work using MC.

Wedges Five-Twelve: Repeat from *.

Wedge Thirteen: Begin at peg 1.

> **Rows 1-33:** Work using MC.
>
> **Rows 34-37:** Work using CC1. Row 37 will place your WY at peg 18.

Working with just pegs 16-18, create a 3-peg I-Cord measuring 2" in length. K2tog on pegs 16 and 17, and continue the I-Cord using only 2 pegs for another 1 ½". K2tog on pegs 17 & 18, and create 5 knit sts on peg 18 only. Trim WY and pull tightly through last loop to secure.

Weave in all ends to secure. The tails can be pulled to the inside of the snake.

Eyes

Using the CC1 BO tail, create a running stitch going through the center cross section of the 2nd short row area that formed the eyelids. Pull these sts to gather the area between the eyes. If you need to tighten up or enhance any sts created during the short rows, to emphasize the eyebrow and eyelid shapes, you can do that with the remaining tail by whipstitching where desired. Another way to do this is by using slip sts with your crochet hook.

The eyes themselves are created with a small amount of contrasting yarn color (sample uses orange). These can either be embroidered into place, or you can crochet two 1½" circles and stitch them into position. You may also prefer to stitch some fun buttons on for eyes to give your snake a more homespun look. The eye detail is added with small embroidered touches, but fabric paint can alternatively be used for this purpose.

Tongue

There are several different ways that you can create your tongue. The sample uses a bit of crochet to sort of free-form the forked shape. Alternately, you can create a 2-peg I-Cord, with the 2 points being made of only 1-peg knit chains (as in completion of end of tail) or you can cut a tongue shape out of crafters felt.

At the very first short-row section of the head, which formed the mouth, push the point inward so that it creates a mouth/smile shape. Stitch the tongue inside this mouth and then stitch the mouth so that it stays tucked inward, shaping as you go.

Finishing

Roll the batting into fairly firm rolls that are larger than the width of your snake. You want it larger, because the stuffing will pack down after time, and you don't want your snake to end up too skinny. It is best to make the roll in one length, if possible, to avoid separation of the batting over time and use. If your batting is not long enough for this, it would be a great idea to stitch the batting lengths required end to end using a sewing thread and needle to secure.

Silly sidewinder, cont.

Once you have your batting roll all ready to go, stuff it into the legs of your toddler tights; half of the roll in one leg and the other half of the roll inserted into the other leg. Add just a bit more stuffing to the areas which will fill out the snake's eyes and cheeks. Trim some of the part of the tights that form the body portion and tuck them around the batting rolls.

Insert your stuffed roll into place inside the snake.

Fluff at the head area, so that the stuffing fills all the right places.

Using a long length of MC, stitch down the length of the snake's body, closing the panels. Work in a zigzag fashion and match the wedges' points to their corresponding outside points as you go.

Also, make sure to tuck all of the wedge's yarn tails inside the snake's body as you seam.

Tie the end of the snake's tail in an over-hand knot.

Steam blocking will help all the wedges lie smooth and straight after seaming.

ELSEWHERE IN THE BOOK ...
Caps and booties

Plush booties,
Page 29

So Cool Cap,
Page 26

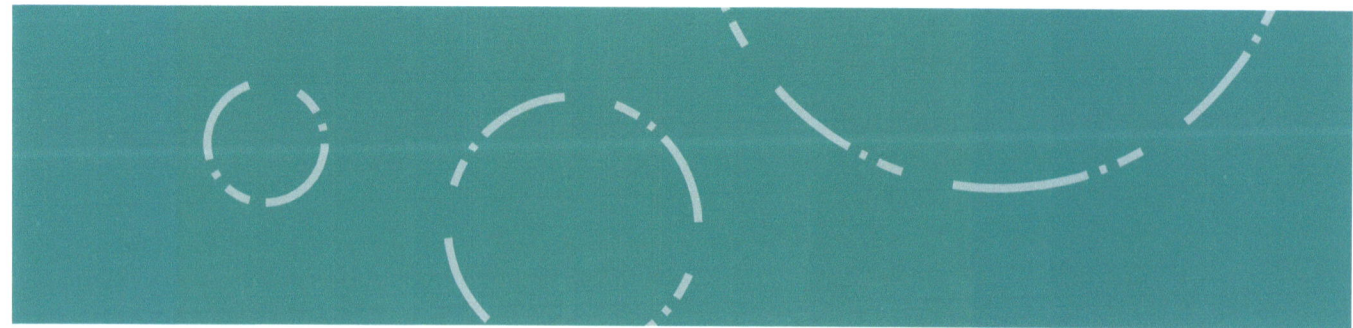

88 Loom Knitting for Little People

Doll Duds

EASY-MODERATE   MEDIUM 4   BULKY 5

It's time to play a little dress-up with those favorite dolls and furry friends! The fun thing about these Doll Duds is that you can mix and match all the projects however you want. You can even make the sweater in a cute girlie color and the skirt will rest right on top of the sweater's bottom trim for an adorable and stylish ensemble.

Bunny's Frilly Skirt

When I was little, one of my favorite things in all the world was to wear a twirl skirt. I just loved to spin as fast as I could and feel the fabric billow around me. Bunny's little skirt is perfect for twirling! Made up of short rows, she doesn't even have to spin to have that ruffled, fresh-fluffed look.

Finished size

2" ruffle height; 10" waist opening circumference; 6.5" total width

Gauge

3 sts (S) x 8 rows (R) per inch

See Gauge and Size Calculators, Page 5

Needed

- Large-gauge loom with at least 6 pegs: pink long 26-peg Knifty Knitter loom used in sample.
- #4 Worsted Weight yarn: approx. 1/8 skein each of 4 coordinating colors of Loops & Threads Impeccable in lavender, dark pink, butterscotch and turquoise used in sample; 100% acrylic, 277 yards per skein.
- Loom tool, crochet hook, tapestry needle

Notes

Techniques used: U-Stitch, Purl, Panel Knit, Short Rows, Crochet CO, Basic BO, Seaming.

For other sizes, just decrease/increase both the pegs used in the wedge CO as needed, as well as the number of wedges worked. This pattern uses one strand of yarn held throughout.

Step by step

Using one of the 4 colors, CCO 6 pegs in a left to right direction. Work as a flat panel.

Work in the following 10-row pattern to create 1 short-row wedge:

Row 1: (right to left) S1, Ust1

Row 2: (left to right) S1, P1

Rows 3: (R-L) S1, Ust2

Row 4: (L-R) S1, P2

Row 5: (R-L) S1, Ust3

Row 6: (L-R) S1, P3

Row 7: (R-L) S1, Ust4

Row 8: (L-R) S1, P4

Row 9: (R-L) S1, Ust5

Drop color — do not cut! — and CO the next color. *(See Makin' it Easy! tip.)*

Row 10: (L-R) S1, P5

Repeat Rows 1-10, building one wedge right on top of the previous one, without binding off or cutting yarns, for a total of 40 wedges.

BBO all pegs, leaving a 12" tail for seaming.

Seam edges of skirt invisibly together. Weave in tails and trim close to work.

MAKIN' IT EASY!

You will be creating sections of short-row wedges, alternating colors with each wedge. When switching colors, there's no need to trim your WY — just be sure to pull the new color to be used up and over the top of all the resting colors. This technique creates a lacy braided edge at the waistline.

Doll Duds, cont.

Rosette Bunny Band

This would be just the thing to make a matching set for a special little someone and her dolly! Just increase the size of the band and you'll have a beautiful girlie accessory for any occasion.

Finished size

Band: 9" circumference, 0.75" wide

Rosette: 1.75" wide x 1" in height

Gauge

3 sts ( ) x 8 rows ( ) per inch

See Gauge and Size Calculators, Page 5

Needed

- Large-gauge loom with at least 12 pegs: pink long 26-peg Knifty Knitter used in sample.
- #4 Worsted Weight yarn: very small portion each of 3 coordinating colors of Loops & Threads Impeccable in dark pink, butterscotch and turquoise used in sample; 100% acrylic, 277 yards per skein.
- Loom tool, crochet hook, tapestry needle, pom-pom maker, scissors

Notes

Techniques used: U-Stitch, Purl, Decreasing, Crochet CO, Basic BO, Decrease BO, Seaming.

For making the headband in other sizes, just increase/decrease both the pegs used in the headband CO as needed, as well as the number of rows worked.

This pattern uses one strand of yarn held throughout.

Make sure to leave approx. 12" BO tails for seaming each piece.

Step by step

Using your headband color, CCO 4 pegs. Work as a flat panel.

Work in the following 2-row pattern until you've reached your desired length:

Row 1: S1, Ust3

Row 2: S1, P2, K1

BBO all pegs. Stitch ends invisibly together.

Rosette

Using your rosette-colored yarn, CCO 12 pegs. Work in a flat panel.

Rows 1-6: Ust all pegs.

DecBO all pegs, roll into a rosette shape, and stitch in place.

Stitch rosette to headband.

Leaf

Using your leaf-colored yarn, CCO 5 pegs. Work as a flat panel.

Rows 1-4: S1, Ust4

Rows 5-7: S1, Dec1, Ust remaining pegs

Gather BO last 2 pegs.

Using a tapestry needle, thread CO tail through bottom edge loops and gather slightly to form a leaf shape. Stitch onto headband, at the base of the rosette.

Weave in all ends and trim close to work.

Doll Duds, cont.

Bear Pull-Over

This cozy little sweater is just the thing to prepare your child's dolls for those chilly ovenings. There are so many possibilities for this little sweater's style...just make it up with different color selections, or add an alternate color-work design, and you've got an entire wardrobe of fashions for playtime!

Finished size

Body: 10" circumference x 5" from neck to bottom hem

Sleeves: 5.5" circumference x 2" in length

Gauge

Body (MC): 3 sts (S) x 6 rows (R) per inch

Trim (CC): 2.5 sts (S) x 4 rows (R) per inch

See Gauge and Size Calculators, Page 5

Needed

- Large-gauge loom with at least 26 pegs: pink long 26-peg Knifty Knitter and loom clips used in sample.
- (MC) #4 Worsted Weight yarn: approx. 1/8th skein of Vanna's Choice Baby, in lamb used in sample; 100% acrylic, 170 yards per skein.
- (CC) #5 Bulky Weight yarn: 1/8th skein of Moda Dea Tweedle Dee in blackberry used in sample; 80% acrylic, 16% wool, 4% other fibers, 142 yards per skein.
- Loom tool, crochet hook, tapestry needle

Notes

Techniques used: E-Wrap, U-Stitch, Purl, Panel Knit, Crochet CO, Basic BO, Seaming.

This pattern uses one strand of yarn held throughout.

Step by step

Body

Using your CC, Crochet CO all 26 pegs to work in the round.

Rows 1-4: Work in the following 2-row pattern:

> **Row a:** EW all pegs.
>
> **Row b:** P all pegs.

Rows 5-12: Using MC, Ust all pegs.

Row 13: BBO peg 1. PFK pegs 2-13.

Rows 14 & 15: PFK pegs 2-13

Row 16 (first color-work row): Still working on just pegs 2-13, Ust all even-numbered pegs using MC. All odd-numbered pegs will be Ust with CC. Twist WY between each st to lock in place.

Rows 17 & 18: Using your MC, PFK pegs 2-13.

Row 19: Still working on just pegs 2-13, Ust all even-numbered pegs using CC. All odd-numbered pegs will be Ust with MC.

Rows 20 & 21: Using your MC, PFK pegs 2-13.

Row 22: Repeat Row 16.

Rows 23-25: Using your MC, PFK pegs 2-13.

Cut WY. Adding a new length of MC, BBO peg 14.

Rows (Back) 13-25: Using MC, PFK pegs 15-26.

Rows 27-30: Using CC, join back in the round and repeat Rows 1-4. On Row 27, CO pegs 1 and 14 that were previously bound off.

BBO all pegs.

Sleeves

Set your loom to an 18 peg configuration using your loom clip. Using your MC, CO all pegs to work in the round, leaving a 20" CO tail for stitching sleeves into sweater.

Rows 1-5: Ust all pegs.

Rows 6-9: Using your CC, work in the following 2-row pattern:

Row a: EW all pegs.

Row b: P all pegs.

BBO all pegs.

Insert sleeves into sweater at armholes and pin. Using long CO tail, stitch sleeves into place. Weave in all tails and trim close to work.

Doll Duds, cont.

Bear Hat

What well-dressed bear is complete without a fun hat to top his noggin'? This hat is a perfect companion to the Pom-pom Hat for kid-sized heads (Page 30). They can be a beary-fine pair in their matching head-gear! Use your Gauge and Size Calculators to make this very same hat in a child-size version too!

Finished size

11" circumference, 6" height (not including pom-poms)

Gauge

2.5 sts (S) x 4 rows (R) per inch

See Gauge and Size Calculators, Page 5

Needed

- Large-gauge loom with at least 26 pegs: pink long 26-peg Knifty Knitter loom used in sample.
- #5 Bulky Weight yarn: MC- 1/3 skein of Moda Dea Tweedle Dee in indigo run; CC- ¼ skein of Moda Dea Tweedle Dee in blackberry used in sample; 80% acrylic, 16% wool, 4% other fibers, 142 yards per skein.
- Loom tool, crochet hook, tapestry needle, pom-pom maker, sharp scissors

Notes

Techniques used: E-Wrap, Crochet CO, Basic BO, Double Knit BO, Seaming, Pom-pom Making.

This pattern uses one strand of yarn held throughout.

Step by step

Using your MC, Crochet CO all 26 pegs to work in the round.

This pattern employs a special color-work technique. You will be wrapping every other peg with the MC, and then wrapping CC on the other set of pegs, for each time around the loom. This gives a fun vertical stripe effect.

Rows 1-10: Work in the following 2-row pattern:

Row a: Using your MC, EW every odd number peg, beginning with peg 1 (keep the WY to the back of the pegs being skipped). KO.

Row b: Using your CC, EW every even-numbered peg, beginning with peg 2 (keep the WY to the back of the pegs being skipped). KO.

Rows 11-15: Using MC, EW all pegs except pegs 2, 6, 10, 14, 18, and 22, as these will be EW'd in CC. At every third peg or so, catch the CC yarn and twist around the MC to lock in place and carry extra yarn length across the inside of the hat.

Rows 16-25: Using MC, EW all pegs.

BO all pegs, using the DKBO method. If you are using a round loom, then BBO all pegs, leaving enough tail for seaming. Press the BO edges flat together and seam.

Create 2 medium pom-poms and attach them securely to each top corner (follow pom-pom maker's instructions).

Weave in all ends and trim close to work.

Steam block thoroughly to soften and mold. It helps to have something round and about 10-11" in circumference, to place your hat onto, so it will dry into the desired size and shape. A Styrofoam ball left in the plastic packaging works great for this!

Note: In the sample, the hat is worn with the bottom section folded up for a textured brim and better fit for the bear. You may wish to decide what fit will work best for your doll and then block it in that way.

Doll Duds, cont.

Bunny Shoes & Bear Booties

No outfit is complete without the right shoes to finish the look. All the dolls and furry critters at your place will be sportin' fancy footwear in no time at all!

Finished size

3" from toe to heel; 7.5" foot circumference; 2" from top of ankle to sole, while on doll.

Gauge

Bunny: 3 sts (S) x 6 rows (R) per inch

Bear: 2.5 sts (S) x 6 rows (R) per inch

See Gauge and Size Calculators, Page 5

Needed

- Large-gauge loom with at least 18 pegs: pink long 26-peg Knifty Knitter loom used in samples.
- Bunny: #4 Worsted Weight yarn: approx. 1/8th skein Loops & Threads Impeccable in lavender used in sample; 100% acrylic, 277 yards per skein.
- Bear: #5 Bulky Weight yarn: 1/8th skein Moda Dea Tweedle Dee in indigo run used in sample; 80% acrylic, 16% wool, 4% other fibers, 142 yards per skein.
- A small length of coordinating yarn is used in both style shoes to create the shoelaces, rosettes and bows.
- Loom tool, crochet hook, tapestry needle

Notes

Techniques used: E-Wrap, U-Stitch, Purl, Panel Knit, Adjustable CO, Basic BO, Decrease BO, Seaming.

This pattern uses one strand of yarn held throughout.

Step by step

Bunny and bear

AdjCO 18 pegs. Work as a flat panel.

Bunny

Rows 1-6: S1, Ust17.

Rows 7-16: Work in the following 2-row pattern:

Row a: Ust all pegs.

Row b: P all pegs.

Bear

Rows 1-10: Work in the following 2-row pattern:

Row a: Ust all pegs.

Row b: P all pegs.

Rows 11-16: Ust all pegs. (no slip sts)

Bunny and bear

BBO pegs 1-6. DecBO pegs 7-12. BBO pegs 13-18. Leave a 12" BO tail for seaming.

Finishing

Using BO tail, seam side edges together until you reach the CO tail. Pull on the CO tail to gather the CO edge until there is a slit opening of 1", formed lengthwise along sole.

Tie the BO and CO tails together in a square knot. Use one of these tails to stitch the 1" slit closed. Pull tails to inside, weave in ends and trim.

Bear

Use coordinating yarn threaded on a tapestry needle to form shoelaces across the front of the Ust'd portion of the shoe. Tie in a bow. Bow ends can be knotted and then trimmed.

Bunny

Using your coordinating yarn threaded on a tapestry needle, create the rosettes and bows with this diagram:

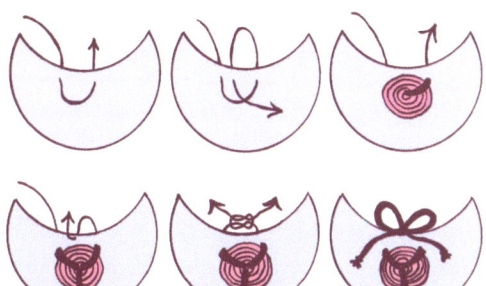

Crazy Caterpillar

MODERATE — BULKY 5

This is the caterpillar version of a crazy quilt! Each ball is a tactile and visual delight, with its very own color and unique stitch pattern. This cuddly companion will inch its way into your child's heart to stay!

Finished size

Each ball is approx. 4.75" long x 11.5" in circumference.

Total length is approx. 44" from nose to tail.

Gauge

3 sts x 5.75 rows per inch

Needed

- Large-gauge adjustable loom with at least 24 pegs: Sample uses pink long 26-peg Knifty Knitter and loom clips.
- #5 Bulky Weight yarn in 5 coordinating colors — approx. ¼-½ skein of each: Lion Brand Baby's First in fairytale, cotton ball, sea sprite, honey bee, and beanstalk used in sample; 55% acrylic, 45% cotton, 120 yards per skein.
- Fiberfill stuffing, 3 pairs of nylon knee highs
- Loom tool, crochet hook, tapestry needle, pom-pom maker
- Optional: puffy fabric paint for applying facial features.

Notes

Techniques used: E-Wrap, U-Stitch, Purl, Drawstring CO, Gathered Row, Increasing/Decreasing, Seaming, Embroidery, Pom-pom Making.

This pattern uses one strand of yarn held throughout.

All Knits are worked as U-Stitches throughout pattern, unless noted otherwise.

Step by step

Ball One

Set your loom to a 24-peg configuration with the loom clips. Using the color that will be the head, DSCO 24 pegs to work in the round.

Rows 1-18: K all pegs.

Rows 19-28: Work in the following 2-row pattern:

   Row a: EW all pegs.

   Row b: P all pegs.

Work a Gathered Row around the loom, as detailed in the diagram. After wrapping, KO each peg with 2 loops. Trim WY, leaving 4" yarn tail to the outside of knitting.

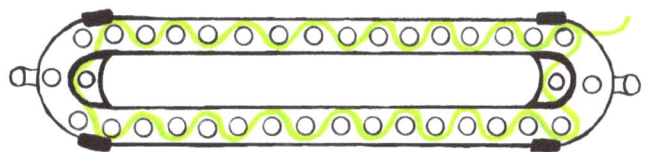

Reach inside the loom and pull up the CO edge. Gather the opening closed tightly and knot. Whipstitch with a yarn needle to close completely. Pull the CO tail to the inside of the work and push the piece back through the center of the loom.

MAKIN' IT EASY!

We will be stuffing this caterpillar as we go. After your first ball is loomed, take one nylon knee high and push fiberfill stuffing down into the toe area. Push the stuffing tightly in, forming a semi-firm ball shape. It will seem like you're adding too much stuffing but the knitting will help settle the stuffing into the correct size. Just remember to keep stuffing about the same amount for each ball. Once you've stuffed the nylon for your first ball, knot the nylon at the top of the stuffing and push the stuffed ball down through your loom and into your first loomed piece. Make sure to keep the remainder of the nylon facing up, as you can stuff at least two balls worth of stuffing into one knee high. Each time you complete looming a ball, reach inside the loom, pull up the remainder of nylon and repeat the procedure. When you've completed two balls, you may pull on the Gathered Row between the first and second balls, to cinch the sections closed, tying the extra length of yarn in a square knot with the CO tail of the new color.

Crazy Caterpillar, cont.

Ball Two

Using the next ball's color of yarn, keep CO tail to the outside of the knitting and work the following pattern in the round:

Rows 1-5: *K3, P3, repeat from *.

Rows 6-10: *P3, K3, repeat from *.

Rows 11-25: Continue in the same method as above, alternating pattern every five rows.

Work a Gathered Row around the loom, as detailed in the diagram. After wrapping, KO each peg with 2 loops. Trim WY, leaving 4" yarn tail to the outside of the knitting.

Stuff your ball, as detailed in Makin' it Easy!

Ball Three

Using the next ball's color of yarn, keep CO tail to the outside of the knitting and work the following pattern in the round:

*Rows 1-6: K all pegs.

Rows 7-10: Repeat the following 2-row pattern:

> **Row a:** EW all pegs.
>
> **Row b:** P all pegs.

Rows 11-20: Repeat from *

Rows 21-26: K all pegs.

Work a Gathered Row around the loom, as detailed in the diagram. After wrapping, KO each peg with 2 loops. Trim WY, leaving 4" yarn tail to the outside of the knitting.

Stuff your ball.

Ball Four

Using the next ball's color of yarn, keep CO tail to the outside of the knitting and work the following pattern in the round:

*Rows 1-5: EW all pegs.

Looking inside the loom, starting at peg 1, count down 4 rows. Pull the loop from the 4th row back up onto the peg. Do this for every odd-numbered peg. KO all pegs with 2 loops. This process makes one row of Popcorn Stitch.

Rows 6-10: EW all pegs.

Pull the loops from the 4th row down from the loom up onto their pegs again, but this time, do this only for all of the even-numbered pegs. KO all pegs with 2 loops.

Rows 11-35: Repeat from *. You should now have 7 rows of Popcorn Stitch.

Work a Gathered Row around the loom, as detailed in the diagram. After wrapping, KO each peg with 2 loops. Trim WY, leaving 4" yarn tail to the outside of the knitting.

Stuff your ball.

Ball Five

Using the next ball's color of yarn, keep CO tail to the outside of the knitting and work the following pattern in the round:

Rows 1-26: *K3, P1, repeat from *

Work a Gathered Row around the loom, as detailed in the diagram. After wrapping, KO each peg with 2 loops. Trim WY, leaving 4" yarn tail to the outside of the

Crazy Caterpillar, cont.

knitting.

Stuff your ball.

Ball Six

Using the next ball's color of yarn, keep CO tail to the outside of the knitting and work following pattern in the round:

Rows 1-26: Repeat the following 4-row pattern:

Rows a & b: *K, P, repeat from *.

Rows c & d: *P, K, repeat from *.

Work a Gathered Row around the loom, as detailed in the diagram. After wrapping, KO each peg with 2 loops. Trim WY, leaving 4" yarn tail to the outside of the knitting.

Stuff your ball.

Ball Seven

Using the next ball's color of yarn, keep CO tail to the outside of the knitting. You will first increase by one peg. At the loom clip, adjust so that you can pull a connecting line from the previous row up onto an empty peg. You will be looming the 7th ball using 25 pegs and working in the round.

Rows 1-26: *K6, P2, repeat from *.

Because you are working with an odd number of pegs, your sts being worked will automatically shift over one peg per row, creating a spiral pattern. Each of your rows will therefore be a little different from the one before — resist the urge to correct this!

After you've completed 26 rows, D1, so that you're back to using 24 pegs on the loom.

Work a Gathered Row around the loom, as detailed in the diagram. After wrapping, KO each peg with 2 loops. Trim WY, leaving 4" yarn tail to the outside of the knitting.

Stuff your ball.

Ball Eight

Using the next ball's color of yarn, keep CO tail to the outside of the knitting and work the following pattern in the round:

*Rows 1-5: P all pegs.

At every odd-numbered peg, starting at peg 1, lift the loop from the peg and hold it in your fingers. Looking to the outside of the work, count down 4 rows from the loop you're holding. Pull the loop from the 4th row back up onto the peg. Replace the loop you're holding back onto the peg as well. Purl the pulled up loop through the loop that was held and replace the pulled loop back on the peg. Do this for every odd-numbered peg. This process makes one row of Reverse Popcorn Stitch.

Jester Hat,
Page 36

Crazy Caterpillar, cont.

Rows 6-10: P all pegs.

Repeat the same process as before: holding a loop, counting down 4 rows, lifting the 4th row's loop back onto the peg, then purling that loop. Only this time, begin with peg 2 and work on every even-numbered peg.

Rows 11-35: Repeat from *. You should now have 7 rows of Reverse Popcorn Stitch.

Work a Gathered Row around the loom, as detailed in the diagram. After wrapping, KO each peg with 2 loops. Trim WY, leaving 4" yarn tail to the outside of the knitting.

Stuff your ball.

Ball Nine

Using the next ball's color of yarn, keep CO tail to the outside of the knitting and work the following pattern in the round:

Rows 1-16: Repeat the following 4-row pattern:

> **Row a:** K1,*P1, K5, repeat from * two more times, K4.
>
> **Row b:** K2, *P1, K5, repeat from * two more times, K3.
>
> **Row c:** K3, *P1, K5, repeat from * two more times, K2
>
> **Row d:** Repeat Row b.

Rows 17-26: Repeat the following 2-row pattern:

> **Row a:** EW all pegs.
>
> **Row b:** P all pegs.

Work a Gathered Row around the loom, as detailed in the diagram. After wrapping, KO each peg with 2 loops. This time, do not trim WY yet!

Stuff your ball.

Tail

Beginning at peg 1, move every other loop over one peg, so that the even-numbered pegs will all have 2 loops on them and the odd-numbered pegs will be empty. K the row, 2 loops over 1, bringing the loops together as you go, so that there are no empty pegs. Move the loom clips as necessary. You should now have 12 pegs with loops.

Trim WY, leaving 4" yarn tail to the outside of knitting.

Using the next ball's color of yarn, keep CO tail to the outside of the knitting and # work following pattern in the round until there are only 4 pegs remaining:

> **Row a:** K all pegs.
>
> **Row b:** P all pegs. Decrease by 2 pegs: one at opposite sides of the round. Move loops and loom clips in as necessary to fill gaps.

Note: *Before the hole gets too small to work through, add just a bit more stuffing to fill out the base section of the tail, knot the nylon and leave any extra in place for additional stuffing through the length of the tail.*

When you have only 4 pegs left, work in this 2-row pattern for 28 rows:

> **Row a:** K all pegs.
>
> **Row b:** P all pegs.

Gather BO all four pegs. #

Cinch the Gathered Row at the base of the tail until it matches the width of the tail and then knot.

Take care of the ends by weaving them in at the Gathered Rows and then pulling them through the balls, to trim on the other side. The tails should slip back into the ball stuffing with a little maneuvering.

Antennae

Using the color that will become the antennae, DSCO onto 12 pegs of the loom, leaving a long enough tail to stitch them onto the head. Work in the round, repeating the instructions given for the tail, between the #'s. You can use a little stuffing, as detailed, or a long length of yarn to fill the antennae.

Make a total of two antennae. Using the CO yarn tail, stitch them in place at the top of the head and at the start of the garter-stitch rows.

Face

You can either embroider the caterpillar's cheeks, or crochet 2" circles and stitch them in place. Following your Pom-pom maker's instructions, create a small pom-pom to be used as the nose and stitch onto the center gathered point of the face. Embroider, or decorate the rest of the caterpillar's features as desired. You can stitch his mouth and eyes in place, or use puffy fabric paint to create his smiley personality.

knitty gritty

Glossary & How-To's

Abbreviation Key

AdjCO — adjustable cast on
BBO — basic bind off
BO — bind off
CC — contrast color
CCO — crochet cast on
CO — cast on
D1 — decrease one
dec. — decrease
DecBO — decreased BO
DK — double knit
DKBO — double knit bind off
DKS — double knit stockinette stitch
DSCO — drawstring cast on
EW — E Wrap
FK — flat knit
HH — half hitch
K2tog — knit 2 together
M1 — make one increase
MC — main color
P2tog — purl 2 together
PK — panel knit
PFK — panel flat knit
rem. — remaining
S1 — slip one
SCO — stockinette cast on
St(s)/st(s) — stitch(es)
Ust — U-stitch
W&T — wrap and turn
YO — yarn over

Basics

Working Yarn (WY): The strand of yarn coming from the main ball or skein of yarn with which you will be creating stitches on your loom.

Casting on

Slip Knot: The first knot to use when adding yarn to your looms. This is an adjustable, easily loosened knot.

Glossary & How-To's, cont.

Half Hitch (HH): This is a simple way to add an additional stitch or two while working a row, as called for in the pattern. It creates a fairly non-loopy, clean-looking edge.

When adding a single HH.

When adding multiple HHs, the extras are applied in this direction.

Then the last HH is as if it was a single HH.

Cast On (CO): A method in which yarn is added to your looms to create a row of base loops from which to begin knitting from.

Crochet Cast On (CCO): Sometimes also referred to as the Chain CO, this is a method of adding yarn to your loom at the beginning of your knitting that provides a finished chain edging. It nicely compliments the Basic Bind Off. This cast on is most commonly used in this book:

A slip knot is added to crochet hook. The crochet hook is then pointed toward the inside of the loom, with the working yarn wrapping around the outside of the first peg, in the direction of the knitting. The working yarn is looped onto crochet hook and pulled through the slip knot to create a new loop on the hook.

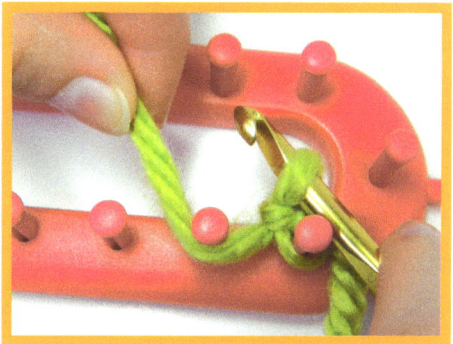

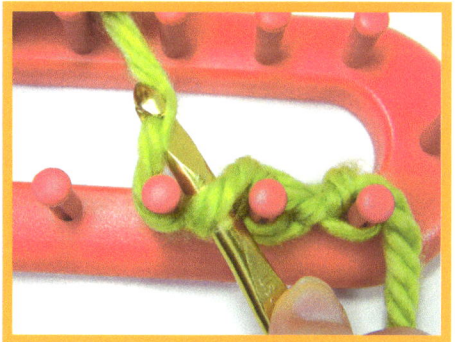

The working yarn is then wrapped around the next peg in line, and the process is repeated. When knitting a panel, when the last peg is reached, the loop on the crochet hook is removed and placed on the last peg. When knitting in the round, cast on to the last peg in the same manner as described above. The new loop created on the crochet hook is then placed on the first peg above the base loop to complete the round. These two loops are knit off, 2 over 1, in the first row.

Glossary & How-To's, cont.

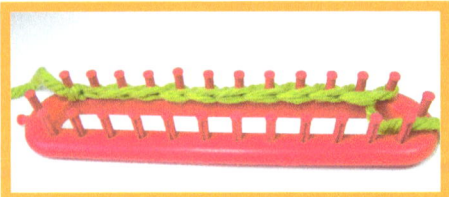

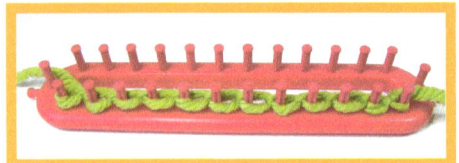

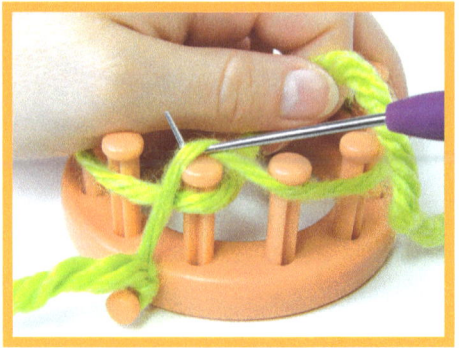

The working yarn is held above the wrapped base yarn on the first peg and the base yarn is knit off.

The result of the Crochet CO is a nicely formed chain running along the inside of the pegs, with a single loop on each of the pegs, as seen from the outside of the loom.

Drawstring Cast On (DSCO): This is an almost magical way to add yarn to your loom when working in the round and you intend for the cast on to be gathered, as in the top of a hat. It is also an excellent way to be able to adjust the tension of your cast-on row. This was created by Brenda Myers and is a favorite technique for many loom knitters:

The working yarn is held aside while the wrapped base yarn is lifted over the next peg in line.

Slip knot is placed on the anchor peg, and the working yarn is then wrapped completely around the outside of the loom in the direction you intend to knit.

These two stitches are repeated, alternating for each peg around the loom. The cast-on tail can be pulled on when called for in the pattern to either adjust the tension, or to cinch in completely.

Glossary & How-To's, cont.

Adjustable Cast On (AdjCO): Also developed by Brenda Myers, this is the technique used for the same purpose as the Drawstring Cast On, but is employed when knitting is worked as a panel, rather than in the round:

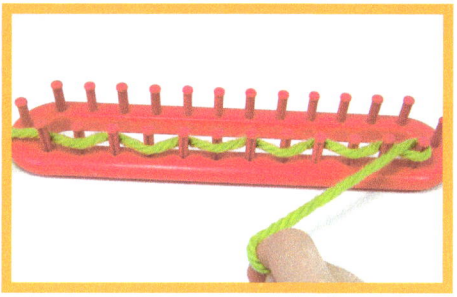

Slip knot is placed on the anchor peg, and the working yarn is then wrapped around the outside of the first peg, and behind the second peg. This is continued, alternating pegs, across the number of pegs being used for the cast on.

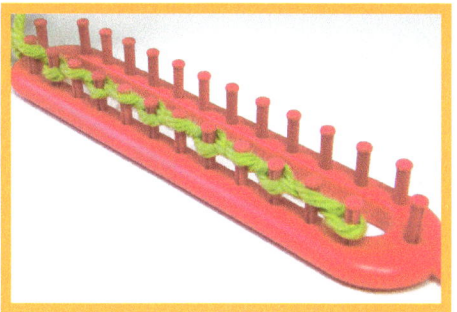

At the turning peg, the working yarn is then used to knit off the pegs with loops, and carry across the outside of the pegs without loops. The next row will be worked as is stated in the pattern. The cast-on tail can be pulled on to either adjust the tension or to gather in the manner called for in the pattern.

Stockinette Cast On (SCO): This method is used to add yarn to your loom when you will be simultaneously using both sides of a long loom, or knitting board, to create a double-thick, two-sided fabric.

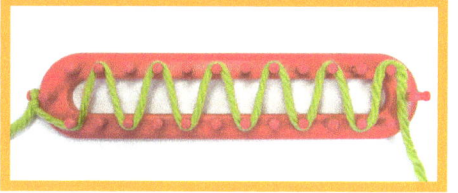

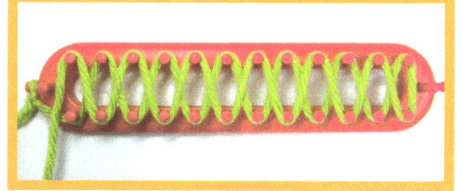

Slip knot is placed on the anchor peg, and the working yarn is then wrapped around the pegs in the manner shown.

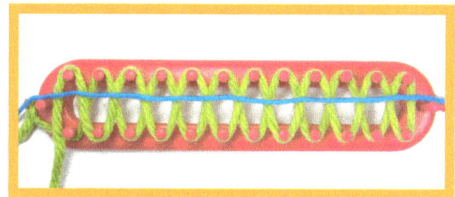

A piece of contrasting waste yarn is placed over the first row of double knit stockinette. It is left there while the remaining rows are worked. This will help you find the correct stitches to complete the finishing part of the stockinette cast-on method.

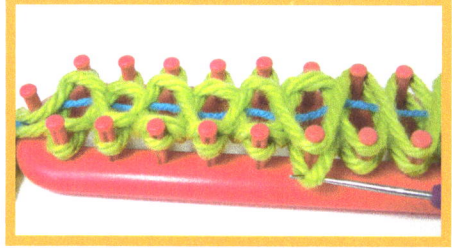

Wrap the loom two times in the manner shown so that there are two loops on each peg. Each of the base loops are then knit off over the top loops.

103

Glossary & How-To's, cont.

Once your knitting has caused the cast-on row to be completely free from the loom, you may finish your cast on loops. This process will create a beautiful non-loopy chain across the edge, which coordinates with the double knit bind off edge. Working from the end opposite the cast on tail, add the first two loops being held by the waste yarn onto your crochet hook. The crochet hook will be pointed toward the knitted piece. Pull the second loop in line through the first loop with your crochet hook. Add the next loop in line and pull it through the base loop left on the crochet hook.

Continue in this manner until you reach the last loop. The cast-on tail is then pulled through the last loop and cinched to secure. You may now remove the waste yarn.

Finished edging.

Stitch techniques

Knit Off (KO): The action of working a stitch in which the base loop is lifted over the working yarn and over the top of the peg.

Slip Stitch (S1): Simply means to not knit, or to skip, this particular peg. The working yarn is carried behind the peg being slipped.

Yarn Over (YO): This is the same as a slip stitch, except the yarn is carried across the front of the peg being skipped.

E Wrap (EW): The working yarn is wrapped around the pegs, with the connecting lines stretching between the pegs to the inside of the loom. Two rows are wrapped, so that there are two "e"-shaped wraps on each peg. The bottom loop is lifted over the top loop and off the top of the peg.

Knit Stitch (K): Working over a row of base loops, the working yarn is laid over the peg, above the base loop. While reaching up through the base loop with the loom tool, the working yarn is snagged and pulled down through the base loop. The newly formed loop is held, while the base loop is lifted off the top of the peg. The newly formed loop is then placed back onto the peg.

Flat Knit (FK): Working over a row of base loops, the working yarn is laid over the peg, above the base loop. The base loop is then lifted over the working yarn and off the top of the peg. This can become rather tight, so use with care.

Glossary & How-To's, cont.

Double Knit Stockinette (DKS): A method of double knitting which creates denser fabric, with both sides made up of all knit stitches. See the Stockinette Cast On for how to create this stitch.

U-Stitch (Ust): Working over a row of base loops, the working yarn is wrapped around the outside of the peg to form a "U" shape, with the working yarn then held pointing to the inside of the loom. The base loop is lifted over the working yarn and off the top of the peg. This is a combination of the knit stitch and the flat stitch. If done correctly, it is one of the speediest ways to knit on the looms, while still maintaining the proper gauge.

Purl (P): The working yarn is laid below the base loop on a peg. While reaching down through the base loop with the loom tool, the working yarn is snagged and pulled up through the base loop. The newly formed loop is held, while the base loop is lifted off the top of the peg. The newly formed loop is then placed back onto the peg. This stitch is exactly the opposite of a knit stitch.

Panel Knit (PK): The method of knitting in which the stitches for each row are worked back and forth, rather than all the way around the loom. This creates a flat piece of knitting.

Panel Flat Knit (PFK): The method of working a flat panel, using either the Flat Stitch or the U-Stitch.

Working in the Round: The method of knitting in which all the pegs of a loom are used and the stitches are connected from the last peg to the first peg. This creates a round, knitted tube.

Double Knit (DK): A method to knit on the looms which creates a double-thick, two-sided fabric. This is done by using both sides simultaneously of a long loom or knitting board.

Extra techniques

Make 1 Increase (M1): Used to increase the number of pegs being used in a row, which will widen your knitted piece. The loops on the outside of the peg for which the increase is called for in the pattern are moved over one, in the direction away from the knitting. The connecting line from the previous knitted row is then pulled up and onto the now empty peg. This line is worked as a normal stitch in the next row.

Decrease (dec. or D1): The manner of knitting two or more loops together to lessen the number of pegs being used, narrowing the width of the knitted piece. The manner of creating the decrease varies and is detailed in each pattern.

I-Cord: This creates a type of cording which can be used for drawstrings, straps, loops, you name it! It is worked using either two or three pegs on a loom. A two-peg I-Cord is created in the following manner:

Place a slip knot on the first peg. Wrap the working yarn around the second peg.

Glossary & How-To's, cont.

Wrap the working yarn around the first and second pegs again.

Each of the base loops are knit off. The process is repeated until the I-Cord has reached the desired length. As you knit the I-Cord, make sure to give it little tugs as you go to keep the tension even throughout. A three peg I-Cord is done using the same method, but with the center peg being E Wrapped each row.

Short-Row Shaping: The method used when you need to create either extra space in your knitting, or a turned section, such as in the heel of a sock. This is created by working a series of decreases and increases, along with a Wrap-and-Turn technique which eliminates holes that would otherwise be created by not knitting the entire row:

At the peg designated to begin your short rows, you will create your first W&T. Lift the loop that is already on the peg and wrap your working yarn from the inside of the loom, around the peg to the outside of the loom. Replace the original loop back onto the peg so that the W&T rests below it.

Knit the row going in the other direction. At the peg designated in the pattern for the W&T, use the same procedure to wrap the peg and turn to work the next short row in the opposite direction.

106 Loom Knitting for Little People

Glossary & How-To's, cont.

You will create your W&T's one peg sooner than the last wrapped peg in the row being worked. These are your decreases. You will usually decrease until you have one third of the original number of short row pegs still left unwrapped or until the pattern states.

When you work your first increase row, simply knit the row to the first W&T peg in line, and knit off the wrapped loop together with the top loop. Turn directions and knit the next row the other way.

At the first W&T peg going in the new direction, knit the wrapped loop with the top loop together as one. Turn directions and knit the next row the other way, including the next W&T peg in the line. Continue in this manner, working one W&T peg each row, until all the wraps have been knit off.

Note: There is another method of increasing at the W&T pegs, in which the first W&T peg is knit off together with the top loop, then an additional W&T is worked on the next peg in line. This peg would then have two wrapped loops and a top loop. The next time this side of the short rows is worked these loops would be knit off three over one. This makes extra certain that there are no holes in the finished project. Since the short rows used in this book's projects that are mostly craft-related, it is up to you which method you choose to employ.

Bind offs

Bind Off (BO): The method of securing your stitches to be able to remove them from the loom.

Basic Bind Off (BBO): This is the most widely used bind off that can be employed for almost any project needing a flat bind off edge. Its chain-like edging coordinates nicely with the Crochet Cast On's edging:

Knit the first two pegs in line. Move the loop from the second peg over one and place above the loop on the first peg and knit off. The loop from the first peg is now moved over to the second peg to fill in the gap.

The loop on the third peg is knit. This loop is now moved over one and placed above the loop on the second peg and knit off. The loop from the second peg is now moved to the third peg to fill in the gap.

This process is continued until each peg is empty. The working yarn is cut and the bind off tail is pulled through the last loop and cinched to secure.

Decreased Bind Off (DecBO): This is worked very similar to the Basic Bind Off, but in this case, two stitches are bound off at once. This creates a gently curving bind off edge, excellent for shaping certain projects:

Knit the first three pegs in line. Move the loop from the second peg over one and place above the loop on the first peg. Move the loop from the third peg over two and place above the loop on the first peg. Knit these loops off two over one. The loop from the first peg is now moved over to the third peg to fill in the gap.

The loops on the fourth and fifth pegs are knit. These loops are now moved over and placed above the loop on the third peg. Knit these off, two loops over one. The loop from the third peg is now moved to the fifth peg to fill in the gap.

This process is continued until each peg is empty. The working yarn is cut and the bind off tail is pulled through the last loop and cinched to secure.

Gathered Bind Off: The method of securing each stitch to be removed from the loom for a knitted piece that is intended on being cinched or gathered, such as in the top of a hat:

107

Glossary & How-To's, cont.

The working yarn is wrapped two times around the loom to measure the bind off length required and then cut. This is then threaded onto a yarn needle.

The yarn needle pulling the working yarn is threaded through each of the loops in line, beginning with the first peg. Each stitch can be released from its peg once it has been sewn through. The bind-off tail can then be pulled and the bind off edge gathered to the desired tension.

Double Knit Bind Off (DKBO): The method of securing and finishing each stitch from both sides of a loom to remove a double knitted piece. This method provides a chained and stretchable bind-off edging.

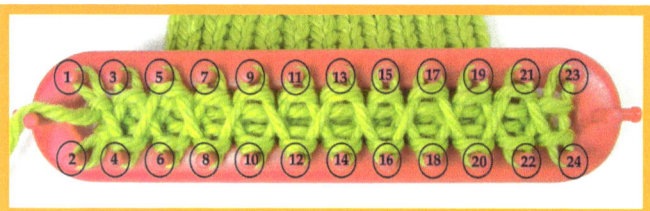

Beginning at the side with your working yarn and at the last stitch to be knit off, use the steps of the Basic Bind Off, but bind off the stitches in the order of the numbered pegs as detailed in the diagram.

Finishing

Seaming: A way to secure two knitted pieces together. This can be done in a variety of ways. You can use a whipstitch, which would attach two pieces of knitting together by using a circular direction around the edges of your pieces with your yarn needle.

Another option is a mattress stitch, which travels up each side of the pieces to be attached in an alternating method. This option creates a bit of a selvage edge on the inside of the seam, but it is nearly invisible from the outside of your project.

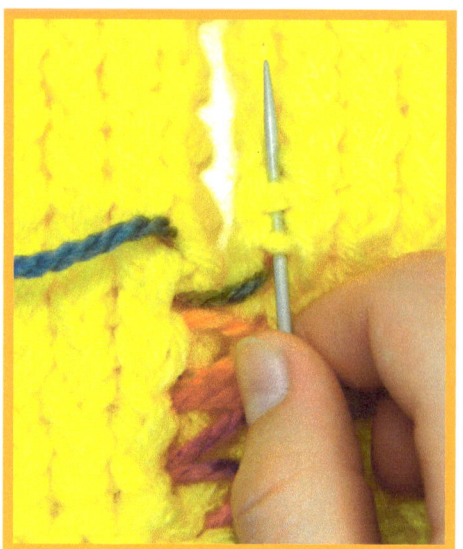

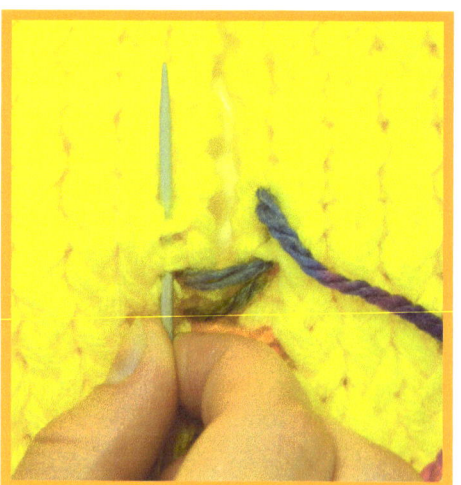

Glossary & How-To's, cont.

Pull gently on stitches until they disappear.

Back side of mattress stitch.

Kitchener Stitch: A method of grafting live loops together from two separate edges of knitting. This is most commonly used in joining the toe of a sock. The easiest way for a non-needle knitter to understand this process is by using the following terms:

To set up your stitches for grafting, divide the live loops into two equal sides. Remove the loops from your loom and place them evenly onto two knitting needles. Hold these needles parallel to one another, with the right sides of the knitting facing outwards.

Note: When working the following instructions, make sure to pull your stitching around the front of the knitting needles, rather than over the top of the needles throughout the process. This makes a clean, nearly invisible graft.

Insert your yarn needle into the first loop on the knitting needle closest to you (FRONT), pulling the yarn needle in the direction TOWARD the knitting.

Insert your yarn needle into the first loop on the knitting needle farthest from you (BACK), pulling the yarn needle in the direction AWAY from the knitting.

Proceed to steps 1-4, repeating them until all the live loops are bound off:

1. Working on the FRONT needle, insert and pull the yarn needle away from the knitting. Slip this loop OFF the knitting needle.

2. Working on the FRONT needle, insert and pull the yarn needle toward the knitting. Keep this loop ON the knitting needle.

3. Working on the BACK needle, insert and pull the yarn needle toward the knitting. Slip this loop OFF the knitting needle.

4. Working on the BACK needle, insert and pull the yarn needle away from the knitting. Keep this loop ON the knitting needle.

When all other stitches have been removed from the knitting needles, the bind-off tail is pulled through the last loop and secured.

Blanket Stitch: A method of finishing an edge with a decorative running stitch.

Glossary & How-To's, cont.

I-Cord Seaming: A method of attaching two knitted pieces together that creates a raised, decorative ridge along the seam. See the Cozy Crib Blanket on Page 69 for instructions.

Weaving In Ends: A method of securing yarn tails that remain from either changing colors, casting on, or binding off. It's best to avoid knots when knitting, as it can be uncomfortable for the wearer, as well as unsightly. When finishing the ends, thread them onto a yarn needle and work them one at a time, through the back layer of the work. It also helps to split the stitches you'll be sewing through with your needle, to help the ends stay secure. First stitch through three or four stitches in one direction, then turn and stitch in the other direction for two more times. You'll be making a sort of "Z" shape. Make sure to pull the stitches in your knitted piece each time you complete a direction, as it will help keep your ends from slipping out when the piece is stretched during use. Trim tails close to work.

Blocking: When a project has been completed, many times it will need the finishing touch that blocking provides. This process helps all those newly created stitches feel more comfortable in their new positions. To block, you can either lightly wash the item as you would normally, then reshape and let air dry (pinning in place, if necessary) or you can steam the item, lightly stretching it into shape as you go. Occasionally check the progress of the piece as it dries to make sure the stitches are setting in the correct position.

Glossary & How-To's, cont.

Felting: Felting is a wonderfully fun process! It turns an oversized, stretchy piece of knitting filled with individual stitches into a thick and woolly piece of fabric that is sturdy enough to be cut through without unraveling. Its uses are many and craft-type projects are at the top of the list.

If you're going to be felting using a washing machine, it's best to place your piece into a zippered laundry bag or knotted pillow case before felting. This protects your project and helps to prevent your washing machine from getting clogged with the extra fiber fluff that tends to gather during this process.

Run your piece through the washing machine's regular cycle with hot water and about a tablespoon of laundry soap. Add a couple pairs of faded jeans for extra agitation. The fibers need to be loosened in the hot water, as well as rubbed together to form the matted fabric you're looking for. Check the piece every 10 minutes or so. Be watchful, because it can felt very quickly and you don't want your piece to process too much and be too small for your project!

The length of felting time varies with different types of yarns and project sizes, but on average it takes between 15 to 30 minutes to reach the desired level of felting. If you check your piece, and the stitches have almost reached the right stage, you can rub them briskly in your hands and in the hot water to help complete the process and avoid accidentally overdoing it in the washing cycle.

The same thing can be accomplished with a little elbow grease and a tub of hot water, if there isn't a washing machine close at hand. Just follow the same instructions and use lots of agitation. You can use a brand new plunger or the bottom of an ice cube tray to help mat those fibers together.

When the project is done to your liking and is the size you intended, gently wring and reshape. Find something that would make a good form for the project. Whatever shape the felted piece dries in, the fibers will set permanently into that shape, so choose wisely. A bowl, container, or scrunched up plastic bags are all good choices. If there is any assembly to be done, it's best to do it now, while the pieces are still damp. That way, the pieces will set permanently into the positions they were intended to be in.

Make sure to check the project regularly as it dries, to ensure that it is retaining the correct shape. Pull and shape the fibers into place as desired.

It will be worth all the watchfulness in the end when you get to use your new, fantastic felted item!

Felted Fun Hat, Page 40

Felted Art Satchel, Page 72

ACKNOWLEDGEMENTS

With a grateful heart ...

When I first embarked upon this adventure, I really had no idea what I was getting into. I figured that if I just dove in, I would intuitively figure out how to swim quickly and with natural ease and grace. After all, this is how I've gotten along in life so far, so why not with this? Well, let me tell you that this has not been the case. I found out quickly that I desperately needed expert swimming coaches and helpful water wings to keep me afloat. The amazing thing is that I had no idea who these helpers would be when I first began. These vital people have shown up along the way, exactly at the moment they were needed most. There's something incredibly amazing about a collaborative effort such as this. It makes me feel so very humbled and hugely blessed to have these people in my life and at my back.

I want to first give appreciation to my sweet family. Without their support and encouragement from the very beginning, you would not be reading this now. My husband endured neglected messes around the house and my attention being constantly pulled to either my knitting looms or my computer. Through it all, he kept believing in me and supporting me to the upmost — my love and gratitude are unending. My two fantastic daughters, Emily and Megan, have been so helpful along every step of the way. They each helped knit samples for the book (Emily knit the Sneaker Slippers and Megan knit the body of the Cozy Crib Blanket.) Emily became our lovely hand model in the How-To's section, as well as being a huge help during the photography sessions. Megan was an enthusiastic helper in the illustrations and in teaching me the finer points of Photoshop. Each of them was a terrific advisor on projects and ideas for the book all along the way. Thank you girlies — you can now have your mom back!

Next, I'd like to send my heartfelt appreciation to the group of gals who've applied their amazing talents and hard work all through the finished piece. Tanya Goen, with Made by Telaine, is a whiz at graphic design. She seemed to know exactly what I envisioned as if she had a computer monitor attached directly to my imagination! She helped set the mood for the book and gave it its whimsical flair. Jennifer Stark (aka: bestest friend eva!) was incredible at finding all my goofs and confusing text — even to the smallest missing comma. She acted as a skillful sounding board for all my ideas and helped me find the best way to put them in place. Thank you, my friend. Christina Flores' camera lens worked its magic throughout this book. Her fresh and playful photos really brought the projects to life in exactly the best way possible! Many thanks to each of you.

A giant thank you goes to our sweet little models and their families for helping with this project! Our book turned out well beyond my imaginings, due in a large part because your kids are such cuties. Thank you so much for sharing them with all of us loom knitters out there!

I want to thank Steve and Ellie Zika, for their compassion in helping widows and their families in Rwanda through their foundation, KidKnits.org, and for becoming an enthusiastic part of this loom-knitting endeavor. Keep up the excellent work!

There turned out to be, along the way, a much larger group of dear people to thank — those who became ardent supporters in helping to get this book off the ground. I want to give abundant appreciation first to Lynn Markman of MarkmanFarm.com. She took this project on as if it were her own and shouldered the responsibility of promoting its launch with her own cheery and giving personality. Many thanks and blessing to you, Lynn! My heartfelt gratitude also belongs to Kelly Jones of KellyKnits.com, Kristen Mangus of GoodKnit Kisses, Tanya Goen and Jenny Stark for being so quick to want to play with the projects of this book and share all about the fun they had in doing so. I deeply enjoyed seeing your creations from the book before anyone else's! Abundant thanks belongs to all those who were so quick to pre-order their copies through our book launch, both because they love loom knitting and because they believed in the project and wanted to be a part of it. Many, many thanks go to each and every one of you.

I'd like to especially thank Isela Phelps, who has over the years been my inspiration, my mentor and my dear loomy friend. Thank you for being there whenever I needed you and for involving me in your loom-knitting endeavors. You rock!

Last, but definitely not least, I want to send appreciation all the followers of my ramblings at GettinItPegged.com. Without you, there would be no book, let alone that extra splash of fun and camaraderie that we share from day to day. I count you all as good friends, even though I have had the opportunity to meet only very few of you face to face. Thank you for being there through the fun times as well as the dull ones. You keep me swimming!

www.ingramcontent.com/pod-product-compliance
Lightning Source LLC
Chambersburg PA
CBHW041959150426
43194CB00002B/62